Problems of Style

SUNY Series in Social and Political Thought
Kenneth Baynes, Editor

Problems of Style

Michel Foucault's
Epistemology

Walter Privitera

Translated by Jean Keller

State University of New York Press

Originally published as *Stilprobleme,* © 1990 Verlag Anton Hain
Meisenheim GmbH, Frankfurt am Main.

Published by
State University of New York Press, Albany

For information, address State University of New York
Press, State University Plaza, Albany, N.Y., 12246

Production by E. Moore
Marketing by Fran Keneston

Library of Congress Cataloging-in-Publication Data

Privitera, Walter, 1954–
    [Stilprobleme. English]
    Problems of style : Michel Foucault's epistemology / Walter
Privitera ; translated by Jean Keller.
        p.   cm. — (SUNY series in social and political thought)
    Includes bibliographical references and index.
    ISBN 0-7914-2333-6 (alk. paper). — ISBN 0-7914-2334-4 (pbk. :
alk. paper)
    1. Foucault, Michel. 2. Bachelard, Gaston, 1884–1962.
3. Knowledge, Theory of—History—20th century. I. Title.
II. Series.
B2430.F724P7512 1995
121'.092—dc20   94-10398
                                                        CIP

10 9 8 7 6 5 4 3 2 1

Contents

Preface

If one wants to explain the fascination that Foucault holds for a public not well-versed in philosophy or history, reference to the role that Foucault's theory played during the collective political and theoretical transformation of leftist thought from the end of the 1960s until today is unavoidable. Among the French thinkers who, though somewhat reductively but not without definitional concision, can be included under the catchword "neostructuralism" or "postmodernism," it is Foucault who was most aware of the Zeitgeist and who could offer the soundest theoretical apparatus for interpreting this restless time.

More than other representatives of "postmodernism," he was able to reconcile radical revisions of his thought with a certain continuity among his critical themes. Antitechnocratic and anti-authoritarian moments, struggles for emancipation or for self-determination on the part of socially marginalized groups, tendencies towards autonomous and aesthetic self-realization, despite the imprecise terminology, these movements frequently found a point of connection, an intuition or—as Foucault himself liked to say—a tool that seemed well-suited to define the current self-understanding and practical projects of social actors. This was not without basis, for despite the detached style of his account, the theory of power, the studies of sexuality, as well as his final writings on the aesthetic of existence were each ultimately situated in the precarious space between theory and practice, where a broad public could recognize the enduring character of his critical engagement.

In this book I will discuss the question of the normative foundations upon which this critical attitude is based. It is the amended version of a dissertation that was submitted to the philosophy department of the J. W. Goethe University of Frankfurt in the summer of 1987.

The philosophy department's Monday Colloquium provided the constant encouragement and stimulation necessary for the development of this work. I thank Axel Honneth and Hauke Brunkhorst for their conversation and advice. John Farrell helped me clarify many problems in numerous, detailed discussions. Finally, the kind enouragement of Jürgen Habermas provided crucial support for the realization of this project.

Last but not least, I want to thank the German Academic Exchange Service (DAAD) for providing the financial basis necessary for this study by granting a two-year stipend.

Preface to the American Edition

This book, now appearing in an unrevised American edition, does not claim to be a comprehensive study of Foucault's theoretical work; rather, it is primarily concerned with his epistemology. Although not many years have passed since the book's completion, the discussion of Foucault has been so animated in the intervening period that many important contributions have enriched this area of inquiry. Nonetheless, I trust that the thesis presented here, which tries to reconstruct the normative presuppositions of Foucault's thought, can still be helpful.

I do not delve into Foucault's material studies in this work; they are only addressed to the degree that this is necessary to develop my line of argumentation. Rather, the pivotal thesis for my study is that the problem of "normative confusions" in Foucault's work can be cleared up, to a large extent, through an analysis of his epistemology. Thus I try to show that the epistemological criteria specified by Bachelard in order to distinguish between critical and traditional epistemology are utilized in Foucault's first studies and, moreover, are retained in implicit form later on, in the transition from the theory of power to a theory of society. Adopting this perspective will make it possible to systematically reconstruct the theory of power in a manner that allows Foucault's critical intentions to be viewed, not as tendencies foreign to his theory, but rather as components that can be integrated into his reflection as a whole. Exposing the implicit normative premises of the theory of power not only results in their increased coherence, but also in rendering them accessible to criticism for the first time.

Another theme that runs throughout the entire book is my critique of the aestheticizing attitude, which leads to all manifestations of culture being reduced to "problems of style" for Foucault. It seems to me that this can play an exemplary role in the discussion of ethical or aesthetic perspectives on individuation.

Introduction

One accusation that has been made frequently against Foucault, especially in the early years, is that the anti-humanism of his theory was incompatible with his public interventions on behalf of minorities and disadvantaged groups. His rejection of all belief in the progress of history, his skepticism regarding the possibility of subjects together producing more rational living conditions in society by way of autonomous practical projects—in short, the thesis of the "end of the individual" with its accompanying resignation[1] vis-à-vis practice were considered irreconcilable with Foucault's engagement as a citizen. Foucault increasingly distanced himself from the Marxist theoretical tradition, moving towards "postmodernism"[2] instead, thereby departing from the Enlightenment's conception of emancipation as overcoming a "self-incurred immaturity." Nevertheless, there can be no doubt about the tenor of Foucault's theory, which does not directly express, but everywhere intimates, something like a promise of happiness.

The enigma of an intellectual divided between scientific distance and utopian pathos can also be seen as an expression of a further *theory-internal* contradiction that affects his theory's understanding of rationality.

On the one hand, there is little to counter the critics who see Foucault's work as one of the most prominent contributions that led the cultural climate, particularly in France, from an emphasis on critique of ideology to a critique of reason. Dismissing him as merely irrational does not lead one to a clear-cut judgment about Foucault's thought, however, because his critique of reason cannot be interpreted as unequivocally irrational. Foucault did not write any aphorisms and did not claim to have privileged access to philosophical knowledge. To the contrary, he valued the argumentative form of his painstakingly composed historical and philosophical writings to the very end, and he formulated his own theory of society. In addition, he always liked to participate in discussions both within and outside of the research community and repeatedly defended his distinctive "rationalism." By bringing together the above-named contradictions, the paradox posed by Foucault emerges in all of its force: A scientist critical of reason and a utopian anti-humanist constructs a fascinating theory without regard to any self-contradiction. These ambivalences serve as the point of departure for the present investigation.

Certainly, the argument that Foucault's theory contains a performative contradiction could suffice on its own to advise against further engagement with this topic. It is significant, however, that even the authors who have gone to some length to point out the missing normative basis of Foucault's critique of reason[3] could not avoid engaging themselves with the content of his theses and with their systematic expressive force. Indeed, part of the task of a comprehensive investigation is to uncover fundamental motifs and to reconstruct implicit presuppositions, thereby furnishing a more detailed understanding of a thesis and making possible a more clearly articulated critique. This project works along these lines. Its goal is to better understand Foucault's conception of rationality in the hope that such a clarification can facilitate both a comprehensive discussion of his work and an immanent critique of it.

Addressing the scientific status of Foucault's theory is especially promising because Foucault's reply to the charge of irrationality stems from this thematic area. Foucault always understood himself as a scientist, even when he described his own theory as "anti-science" and provocatively described his methods as "felicitous positivism" (although his intention thereby was by no means irrationalistic). The responses made by theorists who share an approach similar to Foucault's also rely on the problem of the standard for rationality. The standard response to the objection of those who criticize Foucault's critique of reason as being incompatible with his own theory's claim to truth and who ask about the systematic place from which Foucault spoke is that his critique is concerned precisely with the critique of traditional criteria of justification and that one must first understand Foucault internally before an external judgment can be made.[4]

Naturally, the strategy of claiming that Foucault is "misunderstood" is insufficient to address these questions if it is unable to deliver plausible arguments to the not-yet-initiated that can provide a better explanation of the characteristics of this new understanding of science. This explanation is especially important because Foucault's "anti-science," with its promise of something like an "insurrection of subjugated knowledges" or the conception of a "new economy of pleasures," is tightly interwoven with his theory's latent utopian content. In this respect it accounts for Foucault's compelling attraction.

Scientific understanding and concealed normativity present themselves as a unitary complex to a study that, beyond asserting that Foucault's critique of reason has manifest inconsistencies, wants to investigate the fundamental motifs of his thought in order to examine their strengths. If one privileges the question of the scientific status of Foucault's theory for the reasons mentioned above, then it is advisable to begin by looking at Bachelard's historical epistemology, which Foucault publicly admitted to having adopted in a critical manner. The kinship between Bachelard's and Foucault's epistemology (via the mediation of an author as important to French epistemology as Georges Canguilhem) is by now so well known that it could seem trivial. Particularly in the beginning of the 1970s—in the zenith of structuralism—Althusser and his school, above all others, saw to a rediscovery of Bachelard that established the view that the father of historical epistemology was also a proto-structuralist.[5] In this intellectual climate Foucault's writings, up until *The Archaeology of Knowledge*, were often associated with Bachelard's theory both by commentators and by the author himself.

The recognition of an epistemological line linking Bachelard, Canguilhem, and Foucault suddenly loses its significance when Foucault enters into the period concerned with the theory of power. With this move he adopts a genealogy largely inspired by Nietzsche; as a result, his theory's structuralist motifs are forced into the background. The theory of power is interpreted as a break in Foucault's development. As a result, his entire confrontation with the thematic areas of science, structuralism, and epistemology is seen as useless for understanding Foucault's new developments and therefore is no longer addressed.

In this project I will try to show how Bachelard's epistemology is relevant to Foucault's theory. My approach will seek the lines of connection between the two authors not primarily in the similarity of their structuralist motifs but rather in the continuity of an aesthetic-expressive attitude that is critical of knowledge. That is, I will seek the connection in precisely those aspects of Bachelard which the authors of his structuralist renaissance necessarily had to ignore. The interpretive strategy runs as follows: examination of the hypothesis that Foucault's understanding of science can be traced back to Bachelard's non-structuralist motifs and of whether this line of interpretation is able to consider systematic difficulties in Foucault's work more clearly. If this new reading proves to be the thread connecting Bachelard and Foucault, it can be appraised on the basis of its ability at least to begin to resolve the unresolved contradictions that were depicted at the beginning of this work or, failing that, to represent their systematic necessity.

Naturally, an epistemologically oriented reading of Foucault, like every one-sided interpretive endeavor, commits a certain injustice vis-à-vis the author—especially when he is distinguished by a particularly creative ability to appropriate different cultural spheres. In the case of

Foucault, his thematic affinity to Lévi-Strauss, Nietzsche, Bataille, and Saussure are self-evident, and recent interpretive endeavors that emphasize literary influences[6] or the influence of Heidegger's thought[7] certainly present plausible arguments for their theses. The epistemological Foucault cannot include all aspects of Foucault. Indeed, this particular interpretive proposal does not claim to exhaust the many facets of Foucault's thinking. Rather, it tests one systematic point of view that tries to account for the unity found in the development of his thought in the permanence of a single normative intuition.

In the following I will try to show that the romantic character of Bachelard's epistemology, which is visible above all in his critique of knowledge, as opposed to his structuralist or proto-structuralist motifs, left its stamp on the whole of Foucault's work, not just on the first period, and that it offers a plausible model for interpreting the otherwise puzzling breaks in the course of Foucault's theoretical development. Furthermore, Bachelard's epistemology, so understood, should provide the key to defining the interpretation of science that is hidden in the catchword "anti-science," thereby disclosing the implicit normative premises of Foucault's theory and possibly of his personal engagement, which continued unabated despite his anti-humanist protestations. Finally, the conditions should be created thereby for a critique that not only exposes the untenability of maintaining a critique of reason as a basic attitude but can also discuss the idea of anti-science, with all of its philosophical and normative implications.

Chapter One

Bachelard's Historical Epistemology

The characterization "non-contemporary thinker" conveys the distinctive features of Bachelard's thought while
also taking into account his work's distinctive historical
effect. Bachelard celebrates the great transformations of
twentieth-century physics as no one else. He does this, however, with such complete faith in scientific progress that
his theory—especially in Bergsonian France—appeared to
be a philosophical holdover of the nineteenth century's self-
understanding. The positivistic promotion of science to the
position of the only reliable mode of knowledge, indeed, his
occasional praise of asceticism in research as the ideal for
one's entire life-conduct, are leitmotifs that run throughout his historical epistemology and lend his writings a certain pathos. When we consider the far-reaching changes that
the natural sciences, especially physics, underwent, as well
as the changes in the corresponding philosophical discus-

sions, we can see that many of Bachelard's basic intuitions at the beginning of the century were not isolated phenomena, despite strong opposing philosophical tendencies. Like the thinkers of the Vienna Circle, Bachelard set himself the task of bringing a philosophy that stayed too long in the metaphysical heavens to the standard of the sciences. In the heyday of neo-positivism, however, the strong psychological focus contained in his analyses of the origins of the sciences in research practice prohibited his historical epistemology from gaining a wide reception. Even in the sixties, after the beginning of the so-called "post-empiricist debate," the discussion of the history of science was driven solely by its own steam, without including or even taking note of its French precursor, despite important points of connection with Bachelard's theory. Admittedly, this circumstance and others can be attributed to the fact that Bachelard's large, polemical, and unsystematic body of work does not make easy access possible[1]—and especially not for readers from the Anglo-Saxon tradition.[2]

Even in France Bachelard did not receive the recognition that his influence on the philosophical discussion should have earned him. His epistemology was taken up only later, by the Althusserians.[3] Since then, Bachelard has been discussed from many perspectives. His work is now seen as being relevant to—even the source of—the whole spectrum of theoretical approaches that can be included under the title "structuralism."[4] This suggestion, however, seems even more convincing in the case of Foucault, who explicitly states in his writing that he has utilized Bachelardian themes.

In light of the unsystematic character of Bachelard's work and the limited, solely introductory function that it assumes in the structure of this project, I will forgo a thorough treatment of it here. My depiction will not provide a chronological account of his theoretical development; rather, it will concentrate on the task of examining the thematic connection among several of its aspects. Of course, this approach cannot provide a complete overview of his work, but it can offer a coherent view of his most important epistemological postulates. This inquiry into Bachelard's epistemological theses will provide the interpretive framework from which a selective questioning of Foucault will proceed. On its basis, I will argue that the lack of clarity in many of Foucault's basic epistemological assumptions is connected with the manner of his appropriation of Bachelard's conceptual scheme—and that their dislocation from their original theoretical context into a new one resulted in systematic difficulties that have stubbornly accompanied the entire development of Foucault's theory.

In the following I will sketch out 1) some characteristics of Bachelard's history of science and 2) the critical function of the concept of "construction" with regard to epistemology. From the idea of construction I will develop 3) the themes of pluralism, the applied character of epistemology, and discontinuity. Finally, I will consider 4) the concept of the epistemological obstacle and the relation between scientific and prescientific experience. Thereby I will arrive at 5) a final critique of Bachelard.

Scientific Progress and Traditional Epistemology[5]

If one wanted to trace Bachelard's epistemology back to one basic question that could serve as the guide to his investigations, then this could be formulated as follows: "How is scientific progress possible?" This focus on the growth of scientific knowledge highlights the originality of Bachelard's approach vis-à-vis other epistemological positions in two respects. For one, the history of science takes on relevance as an essential component of scientific theory; for another, Bachelard is skeptical of all attempts to regulate the creative proliferation of knowledge by means of methodically secure procedures. With great polemical effect, sometimes even with anti-philosophical vehemence, Bachelard repeatedly stresses that the great achievements of the sciences are the only form of acquired knowledge that has stood the test of time. Guided by an outlook that shows the influence of Husserl's phenomenology, he repeatedly refers in his writings to those aspects of scientific practice that occur independently of, or even despite, philosophy (where by "philosophy" he means "traditional epistemology"). According to Bachelard, traditional epistemology does not possess its own autonomous theoretical force; historically, it was only capable of hovering in the shadows of scientific reason and parasitically claiming an illegitimate cognitive status for its empty formulas superior to that of the sciences. Since philosophy, for Bachelard, represents an obstacle to scientific progress, the task of the scientific spirit should be, above all, a therapeutic one. As the "superego" of the sciences,[6] reflection should free philosophy from its rigid hypostatizations and should defend scientific growth from prescientific influences.[7] Philosophy, according to Bachelard, should go to school with the sciences. If Bachelard's psychoanalytic metaphor is taken seriously, then we can make a provisional attempt at characterizing the decisive role of the history of science in his epistemology.

Like the psychoanalytic process in which recourse to a diachronic dimension makes self-enlightenment attainable in the present, the retrospective historico-scientific examination of past stages of knowledge serves to guarantee the self-certainty of epistemology. If one agrees with Bachelard that science constantly runs the danger of misunderstanding itself due to philosophical, or more generally, prescientific influences (Bachelard speaks of obstacles[8]), then science can only come into its own by reappropriating its history of asserting its identity in the face of unscientific tendencies. "[E]very philosophy of science must help facilitate access to the modernity of science."[9] This access is a historical one. It shows the complicated connections between theoretical theses and factors external to theory that result in the breaks and discontinuities constitutive of the turbulent history of science.[10] Awareness of the obstacles that have slowed progress in the past allows a more certain acquisition of knowledge in the future.

As will be shown later, Bachelard frequently emphasizes that the history of science does not have a calm, continuous course of development, but rather is composed of radical, unpredictable transformations that lend it more of a revolutionary than an evolutionary character. Nevertheless, his positivistic belief in progress is too strong to allow the thesis of discontinuity to lead to relativistic conclusions. Despite the emphasis on breaks in the actual, historical process, his epistemology proceeds from strong, normative premises that are reflected in a reconstructive developmental logic of the stages of the history of science.

In his book on the formation of the scientific spirit,[11] Bachelard proposes a periodization of the history of science which should help in pinning down the specific character of the modern scientific spirit. He distinguishes, in a phylogenetic manner, among a prescientific period that reaches from classical antiquity through the Renaissance to the seventeenth century; a scientific period, from the eighteenth to the beginning of the twentieth century; and finally the age of the new scientific spirit, whose beginning was announced in 1905 with the theory of relativity.

He undertakes a second classification of the history of science with the aim, as it were, of reconstructing in an ontogenetic manner the specific achievements of the modern scientific spirit. In so doing, he sees in the first, concrete stage the mere curiosity and admiration of a playful spirit confined to the phenomenal level. The second, concrete-abstract stage is typified by a geometric attitude in which geometry represents, as it were, a compromise between the abstract and the concrete; that is, the truth of abstraction is confirmed by sense perception. Pure abstraction, independent of sense perception, is first achieved at the third stage.

Bachelard completes his classification of the scientific stages by placing three psychologically understood interests in a hierarchical relation; these interests determine the affective basis of the corresponding cognitive stages. The primordial, playful, childish soul who admires nature is superseded by the professorial, dogmatic soul who is confined to a sterile repetition of its first abstraction due to its deductive attitude. On the other hand, Bachelard depicts the new scientific spirit's interest at the third stage as a tireless drive to form new hypotheses; the main feature of this drive is the fact that it repeatedly admits to doubt and constantly revises its previous theories.[12]

The thesis regarding the stages of scientific spirit is advanced without making systematic claims and without the support of historical examples. Nevertheless, Bachelard's reconstruction is an undertaking that has a strong normative orientation. Bachelard clearly distinguishes between a merely descriptive and what I would call a reconstructive writing of history:

> I think the history of science should not be an empirical history. It should not be written on the basis of factual bits and crumbs since, in its elevated forms, it is essentially the history of progress in the rational connections of knowledge.[13]

In a move similar to Piaget's developmental logic, Bachelard declares that scientific knowledge, in principle, cannot bring about a regression in knowledge. Regressions and periods of historical decadence can cause science to stagnate or even to be forgotten, but these incidences are merely aspects of a historical dynamic that do not change the logical form of development of historico-scientific processes. Bachelard calls the developmental logic of the sciences "judged history,"[14] thereby referring to the value judgments that the historian of science must make in order to present the logical sequence of the science's truth-content. The question of the normative background which makes "judged history" possible can only be clarified by recourse to the truth-content of modern science.

> Undoubtedly it is knowledge of the past that lights up the path of the sciences. But one can also say that under certain circumstances it is the present which illuminates the past.[15]

The values of modern science, then, are also the values of the history of science, according to Bachelard. For this reason the history of science can never be written once and for all; it changes with the changes in science itself. Every new scientific epoch must write its own history of science. The criterion for reconstructing the sciences' developmental logic can be found in the increasing degree of abstraction of scientific procedures, according to Bachelard. Abstraction, however, must be more closely determined by differentiating between its scientific form and its other forms. In this project Bachelard orients himself on the model of mathematics and mathematical physics; his epistemology's normative content is derived from the description of their procedural method.

Constructions

Microphysics and the theory of relativity set the standards for Bachelard's epistemology. By rupturing the trusted framework of spatial measurement always already assumed by prescientific experience, the advances of modern physics effected an important event, one that should radically transform the methods of procedure both for scientific and philosophical thought.

The result for the natural sciences is that within mathematics, which for Bachelard acts as the model of the scientific disciplines, arithmetic takes priority over geometry. For scientific theory it means that the line of questioning of classical epistemology becomes irrelevant when faced with the revolutionary content of twentieth-century physics. Both the idealistic claim that one can derive the source of truth from the attributes of the epistemological subject and the realistic idea that one can attain a pure access to reality come up empty-handed, according to Bachelard. They constitute two sides to one and the same coin. Their error results from the fact that both ignore the actual procedures whereby the sciences attain knowledge. What they overlook, in his view, is that the mathematicization of the natural sciences implies a new formulation of the subject-object relation. Bachelard uses the concept "construction" to try to interpret for the natural sciences this threshold, the other side of which the traditional epistemological question becomes obsolete.

By "constructions" Bachelard understands the sciences' unique achievement of setting up theories or systems of theories that are not based on prescientific intuitions or metaphysical principles but are supported solely by mathematical calculations and the mathematical systems upheld by these calculations. The scientific spirit has always had a mathematical core. Yet it took the scientific revolution of the twentieth century for it to first be able to assert its autonomy over and against philosophy. According to Bachelard, the task of critical epistemology is to acknowledge construction as the only mode for attaining knowledge and to criticize traditional epistemology's realistic and idealistic variants on the basis of its description.

Bachelard's thesis is convincing. In the earlier stages of development of scientific spirit it could be argued that the scientist investigated a particular, pregiven phenomenon and on the basis of its controlled observation abstracted a lawlike regularity, as it were. But today such a view, given the level of abstraction of the research process, is no longer tenable. It is no longer possible to speak of data as being "given" in the prescientific sense because they are themselves prejudiced by theory. The insight of microphysics, that the phenomenon is inseparable from the conditions of its being recorded, is exemplary in depicting the epistemological status that Bachelard attributes to scientific knowledge. He stresses both that the problematization of theoretical questions results in theory formation and that the object that is the focus of theory construction as such is only conceivable within a theoretical system and is only able to be produced technically with the aid of experimental equipment. "Nature's true order is the order that *we* put into it with the technical means at our disposal."[16] Thus, scientific spirit develops with the assistance of constructions and of experiences that are also constructed and dependent on theory. It proceeds, so to speak, blindly, orienting itself only on the axioms of mathematical physics and on its own experimental equipment. Bachelard points out that the specific achievement of scientific constructions lies in looking beyond the prima facie isolated phenomenon in order to seek relation, to look beyond the simple to the complex. "Application is complication."[17] Changes in scientific thinking are subordinate both to theoretical formations and to the object itself; they make the idea of an immediate access to reality untenable. Reality becomes realization, objectification of theoretical assumptions.

> For a scientific spirit, all knowledge is a response to a question. If there has not been a question, there cannot be any scientific knowledge. Nothing comes from itself. Nothing is given. Everything is constructed.[18]

The concept of construction, understood as the principle that constantly revises and radically reformulates theories, should depict the specific achievement of science in a manner that does justice both to the attainment of knowledge through theoretical structures as well as to the unpredictable revolutionization of these structures. This explanation of scientific practice allows Bachelard to anchor progress in the very definition of science.

The focus on the essential connection between science and progress can also clarify the differences between Bachelard's constructive rationalism and classical rationalism. The development of the sciences can no longer be said to simply change the substance of knowledge; rather, it also changes all spatial and temporal categories, thereby altering the constellation of the subject-object relation. As a result, every a priori commitment to the subject-object relation proves to be nothing but an obstacle for science itself. In the foreword to *The Philosophy of No* Bachelard writes:

The mind [*l'esprit* or spirit] lives by this one piece of evidence. It makes no attempt to create any other evidence. Identification of the mind with *I think* is so clear that the science of this clear consciousness immediately becomes the consciousness of a science, a certainty of founding a philosophy of knowledge. The consciousness of the identity of the mind in all its various portions of knowledge is, in itself alone, the guarantee of a permanent, fundamental, definitive method. In the face of such success, why postulate the necessity of modifying the mind and going in search of new knowledge?[19]

Philosophical rationalism requires revision to the extent that its theses are not able to take into account the abstract, constructive moment of the sciences. In his critique of Descartes,[20] Bachelard stresses that a rationalism that is aware of the state of affairs of the sciences can no longer be based on prescientific foundations because it must have already called into question these foundations and their meaning within the system. If one takes as a given that there are now no more certainties or intuitions which, under the scrutiny of science, would not relinquish their immediacy to the complex network of theoretical relations, then it has been shown that the theoretical constructions developed from the mathematical model are the actual form of scientific knowledge. In this way the axioms presupposed by theory in each case take on a quasi-transcendental significance as conditions of possibility for scientific knowledge. Due to the fact that the scientific object represents a kind of objectification of theory and of the related experimental procedures (as we have seen), according to Bachelard the axioms that replace the naive prescientific intuitions must have a constitutive moment.

One peculiarity of Bachelard's critique of empiricism and rationalism is his vagueness with regard to the tendencies he criticizes. He only rarely concerns himself with one author or with one clearly identifiable school of thought. In most cases empiricism and rationalism appear as two basic psychological options that are described such that they exemplify the intent of the critique. Indeed, Bachelard is not concerned with strengthening or criticizing particular schools within the epistemological tradition. Scientific constructions and experimental equipment give rise not only to a theory's a priori framework but also to its object domain, thereby excluding the relation between the subject and the object of knowledge from their field of experience. As a result the knowledge question, insofar as it can be defined as a problem of the relation between the subject and the object of knowledge, is also excluded since it is seen as a question that is superfluous to the sciences.

Bachelard advocates the necessity of an autonomous science that is discontinuous from life-practice. Thus, he views traditional epistemology and its conceptual apparatus (which originated in prescientific experience) as an undertaking that strove to link science with deceptive ideas arising from prescientific experience, thereby hindering the progress of abstract scientific thought. For this reason Bachelard is also skeptical about the topic of the foundations of the sciences.[21] He points to the apodictic certainty that emerges in mathematics and mathematical physics whenever a new, convincing theory is formulated. Bachelard does not characterize an individual thesis or a set proof as apodictic, but rather a network of relations, a construction that, taken in its entirety, leads to increased coherence. Apodicity is "of a rational order, of a relational order."[22] If one agrees with Bachelard's statement that one always already knows what a good theory is (he points out as an example that most mathematicians demonstrate no interest in the foundations of mathematics), then the question of the acceptability of axiomatic systems and their corresponding theories is by no means left to the arbitrariness of researchers. Rather, their acceptability can be justified apodictically ("apodictic" is understood here on the basis of how coherent they are) in the concrete field of their application by providing plausible theoretical links among theories in the form of contextual constructions.

> The apodictic value thus is revealed more in exten-
> sion than in reduction. The multiplicity of relations
> in some way doubles the evidence, because this mul-
> tiplicity is the evidence from different points of
> view. . . . The superstructure of science strengthens
> the foundation. . . . All solidity is consolidation.[23]

Interregional Rationalism and Discontinuity

Bachelard describes the process of consolidating scientific knowledge with the aid of motifs of thought similar
to those found in the research community.

The agreement of the researchers provides apodictic certainty with its requisite confirmation. The sterile certainty
of the cogito ("I think") is replaced by the permanent discursive renewal of agreement by the cogitamus ("we
think").

> Control, verification, confirmation, psychoanalysis,
> instruction, normativism appear in the I-Thou of
> rationalist thought; all are more or less extended
> forms of co-existence.[24]

Although it is only presented in outline form, the intuition of
the cogitamus clearly indicates that reflective forms of knowing are not precluded by making mathematics the paradigm
of the sciences. Nevertheless, for systematic reasons
Bachelard cannot pursue the implications of the idea of the
cooperative production of knowledge. In order to secure the
autonomy of the scientific process vis-à-vis everyday life,
Bachelard is forced to dispense with propaedeutic considerations regarding the universal, normative presuppositions of
science and to reduce the validity basis of science to the theory-internal, apodictic certainty of construction. He accepts
without reservation the "relativism" that unavoidably results
from this move. That is, he does not see it as an aporia that
must be addressed, but as an appropriate description of the
state of the sciences today that confirms his own approach.

The historical fact that science works with many different axiomatic systems and that, as a result, we are confronted not by one but by many different geometries and kinds of physics and mathematics that constitute a corresponding number of independent object domains, leads Bachelard to develop the thesis of a *regional rationalism* that corresponds to the plurality of theories.

If scientific spirit is not to be confined to the sterility of a metaphysics "this side" of the actual development and multiplication of theories, then scientific rationality itself must be understood as a multiplicity of various regional rationalities. Whereas the philosophical attitude tries to reduce the plurality of phenomena to a unity, research practice shows how every step towards progress and every refinement of its conceptual apparatus and its experimental procedure leads, not to stronger syntheses, but to more progressive differentiation. Far from an increased uniformity among the sciences, Bachelard can confirm his epistemology by pointing to the formation of ever new disciplines. Epistemological pluralism celebrates the differentiation of the sciences as guaranteeing their continual progress. The sciences evolve by distributing themselves into regions of rationality, each with its own language that cannot be translated into a metalanguage. The regional rationalisms are, so to speak, shortsighted forms of rationality that only come into contact with one another through their overlapping spheres of application. Bachelard insists on the dependence of all theory on its experimental context and speaks of *applied rationalism* in this sense. If one separates a theory from its sphere of application in order to extend the validity of its properties beyond its disciplinary borders, then it loses all scientific validity. Due to the applied nature of the sciences, their processes of differentiation, which take place by forming new axiomatic systems or postulates, are not arbitrary. Theory construction follows the rhythm of the revolutions and differentiations within scientific progress; its development is always dependent on a problem area within a particular sphere of application. Thus, Bachelard does not see the new axiomatic systems as positing an immediate and unsubstantiated beginning; rather, as "new beginnings," they are attempts to correct pregiven theories. As both the self-criticism of preceding theories and the preconditions of new theories, they posit as a priori that which they constructed a posteriori from the open questions of preexisting theories.[25] Although Bachelard accounts for the proliferation of axiomatic systems by referring to their applied character and thus to the fact that every new construction is rooted in questions of experimental practice, he is aware that the constitution of scientific regions through the formation of new axiomatic systems implies the execution of radical breaks which, viewed structurally, differ from the "normal" research within an already established theory. Bachelard uses the term *discontinuity* to address the topic of the unpredictable change that occurs with the constitution of new scientific object domains.

Since Bachelard's "applied rationalism" does not permit the formation of metatheories independent of experimental practice, each step towards differentiation in the object domains of knowledge results in discontinuity. According to Bachelard's regional rationalism, the languages of the different theoretical areas are untranslatable; the constitution of a new scientific region always implies a break.[26] Above all, however, discontinuities can be identified diachronically in the history of science, at those critical junctures where the construction of a new theory revolutionizes one's entire understanding of an object domain. The previously mentioned examples from modern physics offer Bachelard sufficient occasion to problematize, as radical upheavals, those occurrences that do not harmoniously fit into a cumulative view of progress.

If one compares Bachelard's interpretation, which attributes a quasi-transcendental status to a theory's axiomatic presuppositions and claims that a new object domain is constituted with the emergence of each new theory, with the numerous instances of unpredictable breaks in

the history of science, then one can see that the discontinuity thesis is a necessary addition to his historical work.
According to Bachelard's history of science, it is not only the
major revolutions in the physics of this century that represent insurmountable breaks. Discontinuities also show
themselves in many less obvious transformations, where
the continuity in the use of a term or a word betrays one or
more changes in meaning to the eye of the historian of science—changes which are conditioned by the further development of scientific knowledge.[27] In the description of the
revolutions that occur in the course of the history of science, or rather, in the fragmentation of the various scientific
domains, the discontinuity thesis represents a plausible—
and, in the complete architectonics of his work, even necessary—component of applied constructivism. But this thesis assumes an even more important role for Bachelard due
to its connection to his concept of construction and thus to
the normative premises of his epistemology.

For a philosophy that sees its main task as explaining
the progress of the sciences, the discontinuity thesis is central because it promises to answer the question of the emergence of the new by way of a further explication. Each construction in the course of the progress of the sciences is an
expression of discontinuity. I use the formulation "expression of discontinuity" here because with this thesis
Bachelard's reflection takes a turn that leaves the field of
experimental research and joins a metaphysics of discontinuous time.[28] In *La dialectique de la durée* Bachelard consciously starts down the metaphysical path by attempting,
so to speak, to stand Bergson's philosophy on its feet. "We
accept almost everything from Bergsonism except continuity."[29] In the critique of Bergson, as always, physics acts as
the model to which Bachelard refers. In particular, he relies
on the quantum mechanical thesis that matter is convertible to energy and that energy is convertible to matter.[30]
From the reversibility of matter and energy Bachelard infers
that if the movement of energy demonstrates a rhythmical
character, matter must do so as well. Matter

is not only sensitive to the rhythms, it *exists*, in all the senses of the word, on the plane of rhythm, and the time in which it develops certain delicate appearances is an undulating time, a time which has only one way of being uniform: the regularity of its frequency.[31]

Bachelard goes so far as to name the vibrated energy "the energy of existence"[32] and draws the conclusion that the "vibrated time" that was attained with the help of quantum physics amounts to the universal and original determination of time altogether. "For us the original time is vibrated time."[33]

The concern here is not to use matter to explain the phenomenon of vibration but the other way around: to use vibration to explain matter. Rhythm is the origin of all possible appearances, from matter to spiritual life, and rhythm is composed of moments; it is a "system of moments."[34] Thus, Bachelard can argue against Bergson's thesis of the primordiality of duration and contend that duration is constructed out of moments. Time becomes a discontinuous sequence of moments, a "rosary without the thread"; "the thread of time is covered with knots."[35]

Aside from this highly questionable attempt to derive a kind of dialectic of nature from the discontinuous character of modern physics, Bachelard's revision of Bergson is interesting because it represents a systematically necessary addition to his epistemology.

Namely, Bachelard's response to the question of progress in the sciences is based on a concept of construction that, lacking further determination, does not seem to be sufficiently substantiated. Bachelard must forgo characterizing the constructive spirit as having definite features of rationality because by doing so he would tacitly reintroduce a kind of a priori reason that would contradict his critique of every nonapplied form of knowledge. In order to avoid compromising the principles of his epistemology and yet be able to claim that knowledge by way of constructions that surpass the contingency of historical examples is the normative method of procedure for scientific spirit, he must rely on an achievement that, without possessing a priori features that could be isolated even before application in concrete scientific areas, can be reflected in the many forms of scientific rational construction. To the degree that this is accomplished, this achievement can be understood as a rational force. Bachelard defines this supple rational or rationality-producing force on the basis of his critiques of Bergson's conception of time.

According to Bachelard, the *philosophie de la durée* is not only incapable of thinking the revolutionary emergence of the new;

> the philosophy of the *élan vital* has not been able to give its full meaning to what we will call the purely ontological success of being, that is, to the renewed creation of being by itself, in the intellectual act of consciousness.[36]

The new can be thought successfully, however, within the framework of a discontinuous metaphysics of time. Within this framework are found the philosophical premises that permit the moment of creative (*kreativ*) construction so indispensable to scientific spirit to be traced back to a creative (*schöpferische*) force that produces the new creatively (*kreativ*) and in an unpredictable manner. In this way Bachelard finally arrives at an idealistic sublimation of vitalism.[37] The scientific spirit, with its constant transgression of scientific theories, becomes the highest form of expression of the human and of the universal rhythmic being. His passionate formulation of this unique mix of Bergsonian influences and scientific themes conveys the driving force this intuition has for his philosophy.

> For isn't the brain the true center of human evolution, the terminal bud of the vital spirit? . . . By what light do we recognize the importance of these sudden syntheses? By an ineffable light that brings security

and happiness to our minds. This intellectual happiness is the first sign of progress. . . . Understanding has a dynamic dimension; it is a spiritual élan, a vital élan.[38]

The application of Bergsonian terminology by an author like Bachelard should not be taken too literally since, for rhetorical purposes, he takes great liberties in using expressions from other philosophies. Nevertheless, his frequent recourse to terms like "energy," "force," or "activity" is informative with regard to his characterization of the scientific spirit. As a result, it seems appropriate to characterize his epistemology as a "romanticism of intelligence."[39] The scientific spirit expresses an idea of "living thought"[40] that always surpasses itself. The structure of scientific spirit, according to Bachelard, "changes"[41]; its progressive orientation stems from this changeable structure as well as the "openness" of an epistemology that is aware of the procedure of scientific spirit and that, like the sciences, functions by constantly contradicting earlier knowledges.[42] Against this background Bachelard composes his portrait of a philosophy that remains on a prefallibile level and that, due to its closed nature, must ignore the theoretical significance of scientific progress.

The Epistemological Obstacle

Coming to terms with the problem of philosophy's perpetual "late arrival" vis-à-vis the sciences is a motif that has always permeated Bachelard's thought. He regards the philosophical, or rather, the epistemological, line of questioning as a stubborn perversion of pure scientific rationality that cannot be overcome once and for all. Moreover, it often leads to a distortion or misperception of the specific character of the sciences, including the scientist's own self-understanding.

But philosophy is only one aspect of a prescientific experience that also expresses its substance in the cognitive

habits of daily life, in poetry, and in the imaginative products of the sensible world. According to Bachelard, the imaginative capacity is an indispensable aspect of intellectual
life that intersects with the abstractive achievement of the
sciences.[43] For him the imaginary is related to science just as
the unconscious is related to the ego. Therefore, he finds it
necessary to subject the tension between scientific thought
and prescientific experience to a "psychoanalysis of objective knowledge" that should free the development of scientific abstraction from its mortgage to prescientific contents. Bachelard calls the many moments that repeatedly
interfere with the pure development of scientific spirit *epistemological obstacles*.

Nourished by a daily life laden with prejudices, epistemological obstacles rely on an instinct of preservation[44] that
prefers the comfortable confirmation of the already known
to the *élan vital* of the constructive spirit. Bachelard's psychoanalysis of the objective spirit internalizes, as it were,
the knowledge problematic. Here it is not a matter of the
relation between the subject and the object of knowledge
but rather of the inner-psychic conflict between scientifically proven constructions and trusted ideas from daily life
or from the cultural tradition. What distinguishes scientific
content from epistemological obstacles is their respective
relation to sense perception. While mathematics introduces
a knowing of pure relation, philosophy and the unprob-
lematized ideas from everyday life are limited to perceptions which are unable to produce knowledge as such.
Evidence from the world of perception is deceptive because
perceptions are an active achievement that carry the stamp
of both imaginary and unconscious motivations. Thus,
sense perception merely represents forms of expression of
the unconscious—as do the philosophies whose conceptual
apparatuses, despite their higher level of abstraction, easily betray their origin in prescientific experience.
Epistemological obstacles, like the sciences, are structured
and constructed, but while scientific constructions, as pure
forms of relation, represent the conscious form of abstract

rationality, epistemological obstacles have a status that more closely approximates that of rationalizations. They are firmly established opinions that misunderstand their own constructed status and are satisfied with the deceptive immediacy of their evidence. The substance of knowledge arises from the unconscious production of the prescientific spirit from which, so to speak, the scientific spirit differentiates and delimits itself. Seen as an epistemological obstacle, this substance forms the negative, prejudicial, and yet necessary background for the emergence of science. "When it [scientific spirit] encounters scientific culture, it is never young. It is even very old, because it is as old as its prejudices."[45] Thus, epistemological obstacles are not external factors that disturb the development of the sciences; rather, they belong to its very structure, serving as the negative background against which the history of the implementation of scientific rationality is played out.[46]

In order to classify the epistemological obstacles found in Bachelard's scientific theory, we can set up one schema with three tiers that correspond to the three basic modes of knowledge. Those forms of knowledge are placed at the first, lowest stage that, according to Bachelard, are of interest to life and that comprise the sphere of everyday experience. There, in immediate proximity to perceptions and instances of practical life, authentic cognitive interests must be sacrificed for the benefit of inclinations or needs that impair the cognitive validity of their constructions. They represent the most simple and immediate form of epistemological obstacle.

> To connect the two interests, interest to life and interest to spirit, by means of a vague pragmatism, is to unite two opposites arbitrarily. It is the business of the psychoanalysis of the scientific spirit to distinguish these two opposites and to break the solidarity of spirit with the interests of life.[47]

Unreflective forms of knowing, such as opinion, belong to the first stage which, together with perceptions, Bachelard places below the epistemological threshold. "Opinion thinks incorrectly; it translates needs into knowledge."[48]

Epistemological obstacles of another kind operate at the second stage of knowledge. Philosophy is the most important representative here. Unlike the immediate forms of knowing characteristic of life interests, philosophy raises a theoretical claim, thereby placing itself on the other side of the epistemological threshold. But unlike the mathematical form of scientific spirit, which is found at the third stage, philosophy forms, as it were, a compromise between science and everyday life. Philosophy finds itself in the position of the naive scientific spirit that is characterized by the inclination to reduce laws and facts, the abstract and the concrete, to one common denominator, as well as to present scientific findings pictorially, in the form of quasi-perceptible evidence. Dominique Lecourt thus correctly, in this context, defined philosophical obstacles by their function: to introduce extrascientific values into science, thereby covering up the radical break between the sciences and everyday life.[49]

The break between scientific and prescientific knowing is in fact the decisive motif in Bachelard's thought; it allows systematic status to be attributed to epistemological obstacles. To resort to the psychoanalytic metaphor once again (and Bachelard provides sufficient occasion for that): In their immediate, everyday, or philosophical form epistemological obstacles can be understood as the id or superego, respectively, of a mathematical scientific spirit that always runs the danger of misunderstanding the discontinuity between the scientific and the sensible world and thus engaging in false instances of mediation. For that reason it is the task of a psychoanalysis of objective spirit to investigate the structure of epistemological obstacles; to seek the motivational basis behind their necessary intersection with science in the unconscious, imaginary production of the human spirit; and in this way to hold night and day, reason and dream, asunder. This task is advocated emphatically by Bachelard not only as a useful precondition for the development of the sciences; it sometimes seems to carry even an ethical valence for his philosophical discourse as a whole. The duty of the reasonable person seems to consist in taking leave of the sensible world and in conquering the materiality of life: "Pure thought should begin as a rejection of life."[50]

Actually one can hardly expect something else from a way of thinking that locates the true, living strength of human persons in the mathematical ingenuity of the creative spirit and that reduces the representations of everyday life to a mere unconscious ossification of intelligence. The reversal that turns the symbolically prestructured experience of everyday life into appearance and scientific creativity into human essence must then, as a result, join an asceticism of the "living intelligence" that has as its normative ideal the utopia of a kind of "erudite republic." "Then the social interests will finally be reversed: society will be there for the school and not the school for society."[51]

Bachelard's Philosophy

It would not be easy to find a contemporary philosopher who worked as diligently as Bachelard on the program of adapting philosophy to the standards of the sciences. Nevertheless, Bachelard is not actually a scientist. His basic concern is a critical one; thus, in order for epistemology to fulfill its function as guardian of the sciences he must take recourse in an extrascientific moment. "The mind [spirit] may change its metaphysics, it cannot do without metaphysics."[52] Although his work frequently construes arithmetic, due to its purely constructive character, as central to each form of rationality, Bachelard does not renounce the task of clearly separating the sphere of the sciences from that which, without further specification, we would call philosophy.

Philosophy's foundational role appears, among other places, in Bachelard's architectonics, which is characterized by a duality between science and imaginative production. Most commentators tend to view Bachelard only as a theorist of science and see his preoccupation with these two thematic areas, between which his life-work oscillates with surprising regularity, as a private peculiarity, an aspect of his individual character. To the contrary, Michel Vadée shows that the epistemological and critical literary themes of Bachelard's work first become completely consistent when they are viewed from a unified philosophical perspective.[53] Jean Hyppolite has remarked[54] that both of these thematic areas can be traced back to one basic philosophical thought that is related to the themes of Romanticism.[55] An "ontic-ontological" imagination[56] is operative at the source of science and poetry, prior to their divergence; its creative nature represents their a priori openness to the future. In this topos can be found the basic intuition that links the creation of poetry with the productivity of the sciences, thereby making possible an understanding of Bachelard's oeuvre as a systematic unity. For epistemology in particular, the idea of the creative imagination enables the vital question of the possibility of scientific progress to be placed within a plausible framework.

If Hyppolite's interpretation is correct, then suddenly Bachelard's philosophy seems to be a last attempt to resolve the problematic of the modern sciences philosophically, which entails, for Bachelard, integrating the scientific forms of rationality into the framework of an idealistic philosophy of consciousness. For all that, Bachelard is in the peculiar position of only being able to avoid some of scientism's aporias due to the imprecision of his metaphysics. It would be problematic to defend his arithmetical model of reason if the productivity of spirit could not also secure a place for a plurality of *other* forms of rationality within his epistemology, such as the reconstructive elements in the history of science, the adoption of psychoanalysis, the theory of epistemological obstacles, as well as the vague suggestions of a possible intersubjective anchoring for his theory of science. These are all aspects of rationality that reach far beyond the boundaries of mathematical calculation and that have no systematic basis for Bachelard beyond this: They are forms of expression of scientific spirit. Thus, with its polymorphous character, spirit is that moment under which all the forms of rationality can be gathered that are omitted from the standard of the positivistic empirical sciences.

But the attempt to compensate for the reflective deficit of the sciences by resorting to the supple force of the imagination cannot convincingly supplement the scientific forms of rationality because this discussion of imagination remains too undifferentiated. In fact, historical reconstruction and psychoanalysis remain on the level of mere application; they are silently recognized as rational undertakings without the background of their own rational features being questioned. As the form of expression of a "living thinking," they serve to fill in the gaps of a reductionistic epistemology, but with regard to their own rational characteristics they are misunderstood. The Bachelardian spirit remains a metaphor for instances of reason that Bachelard cannot express in any other way. Indeed, he must retain an undifferentiated account of spirit because recognizing additional rational features in the reflective forms of knowing used in his empirical investigations would call into question the monopoly of mathematical construction as the model of science in general.

Bachelard's epistemology must banish its critical moments to the indeterminancy of spirit's supple power. This includes psychoanalysis, which acts as the framework for other aspects of his theory.

In the following treatment of Foucault's theory, I will try to show how Bachelard's epistemology can illuminate many aspects of Foucault's problematic. I will take the concept of scientific spirit as the point of departure for a specification of the sphere that Foucault calls the "historical a priori." By so doing, I will analyze the function that some of Bachelard's concepts, such as construction, discontinuity, and regional rationality, take on for the Foucauldian variant of structuralism. Furthermore, I will analyze the consequences that result from adopting Bachelard's way of thought while renouncing the central theme of the creative subjectivity of spirit. I will argue thereby that this renunci-ation and the related endeavor of defining subjectivity, not as a premise for the production of knowledge but as its his-torical product, result in the stubborn aporias which shed light on the inner reasons for the thematic shifts found in the different periods of Foucault's thought.

Chapter Two

Foucault: The Early Writings and the Structuralist Period

Michel Foucault's way of thinking is somewhat puzzling. It is difficult to avoid a certain confusion if one looks beyond his various thought-provoking ideas and the fascinating, unforeseen evidence of his material investigations and instead seeks motifs that would constitute his philosophy as a coherent whole. What is most striking in his work are the abrupt turns and the thematic shifts which the author, with a sovereign gesture, hardly bothers to justify. That is why so many different readings of his theory have found their legitimate basis in the various periods of his thought; epistemological-structural,[1] vitalistic,[2] and Heideggerian readings[3] have succeeded one another in the course of the years and have only recently been related to each other in comprehensive studies.[4]

Within the framework of these attempts to grasp Foucault's theory as a systematic unity, it can prove useful to renew the search for Bachelardian motifs in Foucault's work, but from a non-structuralist perspective. Bachelard failed to establish a school of thought in the sense of a group of theorists consciously taking up his approach as the framework or point of departure for their own work. He won recognition for a series of attitudes and procedural methods, however, that have been reflected in the French consciousness to a large extent.[5]

The intention here is not, of course, to dispute the strong structuralist and (later, under the influence of Nietzsche) genealogical features of Foucault's theory. They are too striking and too universally substantiated for the consensus over them to be questioned seriously. Rather, I intend to show that some of Bachelard's intuitions play an important role as the theoretical background or intellectual habit that shapes the Foucauldian *appropriation* of structuralist, genealogical, and even ethical motifs.

Such a project runs into one principal difficulty. The postulation of a theoretical attitude that quasi-unconsciously leaves its stamp on a thinker's intellectual development in some relevant way may suggest room for further thought, but it certainly cannot be substantiated easily. It can even run the risk of illegitimately cutting the thinker's theory short. For this reason, after presenting all Foucault's explicit references to Bachelard's philosophy, I will choose an indirect path. I will try to show that Bachelard's epistemology, and the aspects of it that are concerned with theory constitution in particular, represent the least common denominator that can be traced throughout the various periods of Foucault's theory. It is a denominator that can do justice to Foucault's specific, and in many cases atypical and aporetic, appropriation of philosophical approaches. If I am successful in using Bachelard to identify, in one epistemological leitmotif, both the uniqueness of Foucault's appropriation of Saussure and Nietzsche and to identify the source of the lacunae in Foucault's hybrid form of structuralism or genealogy, it may be possible to come to a unitary understanding of the apparent breaks in the development of Foucault's thought and to develop a comprehensive critique of his approach.

Before I address Foucault, however, I would like to call to mind in summarized form some of the themes in Bachelard's thought so that the concerns with which I question Foucault will be clear. They can be listed under three points.

1. Bachelard's critical epistemology is based on the conceptual pair scientific construction/traditional epistemology. Traditional epistemology starts from the premise that a profound substantive truth, which acts as a source of knowledge, can be located in either the object or the subject of knowledge. Thus, whereas this approach must be satisfied with sterile certainties incapable of progress, for Bachelard scientific construction secures the only possible path whereby progress can be made in the production of knowledge. Scientific construction is understood as scientific practice which, like labor for Marx, should offer a way out of the line of questioning of traditional epistemology. The problem of an immediate relation between subject and object no longer arises for Bachelard. For him, critical epistemology's acts of theory formation take on constitutive status in the history of science and allow new scientific objects to appear in each case. As I would like to show, the topic of scientific construction versus traditional epistemology presents itself as the guide to the entire range of Foucault's thought.

2. Bachelard advocates a highly original variant of Bergsonian vitalism, the substance of which might be rendered by the term "ascetic vitalism."[6] The "will to knowledge" of scientific spirit is ascetic because it completes an epistemological break from the knowledge of everyday life, which has been denigrated to the status of an epistemological obstacle. Thereby, in a curious reversal of vitalism, lifeworld relations become the ossified remainder of spirit's abstractive endeavors, which are

understood as the true life form. The traces of this motif can also be found in Foucault.

3. Bachelard's philosophy or "metaphysics," that is, his romantic conception of subjectivity as ontic-ontological imagination,[7] will allow access to a reading of Foucault which, like a hidden leitmotif, makes the discontinuous development of his theory more understandable. Explicit clues for this reading are offered in Foucault's first work.

The romantic interpretation of Bachelard is by no means uncontested. To the contrary: Most interpreters, especially the Althusser School[8] with its representatives in Germany[9] and Italy,[10] have attempted to play Bachelard's purely epistemological theses off against the metaphysical part, which is held to be marginal. Counter to this reading, dominant in the 1970s, Hyppolite and Vadée have argued, convincingly to my mind, that without the metaphysical background Bachelard's thought loses its coherence.[11]

In his first major works in particular, it is clear that Foucault's reception of Bachelard lies within the structuralist line of interpretation, which had to reject concepts with a strong psychological stamp, such as "scientific spirit" or "psychoanalysis of objective knowledge." Several indicators suggest, however, that the "decapitated" Bachelard of the structuralists cannot be reconciled easily with Foucault's reception of him and that the romantic motif of a pre-individualistic subjectivity, understood as a stream of the imaginary, forms the philosophical framework for Bachelard's epistemology as well as remaining a central intuition for Foucault.

Support for this thesis can be found in Foucault's first article, the foreword to the French edition of Binswanger's *Le rêve et l'existence*.

Dream Analysis

Despite theoretical references and a terminology that Foucault later drops, the foreword to Binswanger's *Le rêve et l'existence*[12] probably offers the most pithy synthesis of Foucault's basic philosophical intuitions.

Both the thrust and the polemical objectives of his later works are first formulated here. Foucault views Freud and Husserl as necessary guides to, but also as obstacles to, the development of a still unfolding "anthropology of expression." Expressive acts—according to Foucault—were, in a sense, made the center of their own thematic area by psychoanalysis and phenomenology; yet this was done in a more or less reductive manner, which did not do justice to the "plenitude" of their philosophical significance. Freud's *Interpretation of Dreams* is criticized from the point of view that it ignores the "imaginary" dimension of "meaningful expression."[13] According to Foucault's reading, Freud analyzes dream language solely in its semantic, not in its morphological and syntactic, functions.[14] The dream seems to be restricted to the level of parole—a level which systematically excludes every regularity from consideration so that instead of articulating the structures of the imaginary, all that remains accessible to psychoanalysis is an indeterminate concept of desire or will. "Freud caused the world of the imaginary to be inhabited by Desire as classical metaphysics caused the world of physics to be inhabited by Divine Will and Understanding."[15] Foucault levels a similar critique against Husserl. By examining the problem of expression in terms of intentionality, phenomenology too narrowly construes its object domain. With regard to the problem of expressivity, Freud and Husserl are brought to one common denominator; of particular interest here is the kind of critique that is made against both of them. It is a fundamental epistemological critique that follows the model of Bachelard's critique of traditional epistemology. Desire in psychoanalysis and intentionality in phenomenology are to be criticized because, in the epistemological analysis of expressivity, they take on the same status that naively and realistically conceived natural objects possessed in prescientific attempts at explanation. Like epistemological obstacles, they embody underlying instances that, by being revealed as the essence of expression and as the immediate source of its truth, conceal the relational character of expression itself. Just as Bachelard's scientific spirit sought a web of abstract relations which could be scientifically constructed behind the apparent primordiality of substance and attributes, so is Foucault's analysis critical of realism. This is demonstrated by the fact that it orients itself on the search for a grammar of expressivity.

But above and beyond providing a critique of psychoanalysis, dream analysis serves as the place where Foucault can formulate his own approach, if not completely, at least in a provisional, intuitive form. "Freud," he writes, "psychologized the dream."[16] He remained trapped in the conceptual schema of a psychological tradition that, by denigrating the dream to a merry-go-round of images, was unable to find access to the actual phenomenon of expression. But the dream is precisely the critical place where the limitations of the above-mentioned reduction of expressivity is most visible. Foucault points to a conception of dreams, rich in tradition, that exists alongside the psychological, ego-centered dream analysis; it can elucidate the epistemological level of an anthropology of expression.

Contrary to the search for meaning that characterizes "psychological" dream analysis, an understanding of the dream as dream experience (expérience onirique) can be documented that dates back to Greco-Roman culture. Foucault does not economize on cultural-historical examples here. He sees running through Heraclitus, classical tragedy, and some currents in Christian theology and the Renaissance[17] the historical thread of an intuition which, bound up as it is with problems such as fate or mercy, represents only some of the stages of a quite wide-ranging history of the dream. Throughout this history, however, the dream is recognized as a privileged source of knowledge.

The epoch in which this motif is taken up in a number of different forms, however, is Romanticism. By referring to Schelling, Novalis, Baader, and Schleiermacher, Foucault tries to track down the literary, philosophical, and mystical

variants on an intuition of the dream as original experience.[18] This experience delineates an area that precedes the
conceptual pairs of transcendence and immanence, subjectivity and objectivity. The region of oneiric experience is
one of "radical subjectivity"[19]; identity cannot be attributed
to it.

> [T]he subject of the dream is not so much the per-
> sonage who says "I" . . . as the whole dream in the
> entirety of its dream content. The subject of the
> dream, the first person of the dream, is the dream
> itself, the whole dream.[20]

In his analysis Foucault vacillates between a conception of
the dream as experience and the idea that the dream is
accessible to a structural description. As we will see, this
ambivalence will pervade Foucault's thought for a long time
to come. Central to this essay, in any case, is the critique of
traditional epistemology's subject-object line of questioning in favor of the productivity of the pre-individualistic,
creative character of the imaginary.[21]

If one views this reading of Foucault's dream conception retrospectively, from the perspective of his later works,
it appears to be a still insufficient, yet nonetheless immediately exemplary and quasi-visual depiction of that which
will later be called discourse or power. As a region neither
ideal nor material that is both self-creating and self-forming,
the dream is an excellent example of "differential transcen-
dentalism,"[22] that unique model of theory constitution that
Foucault repeatedly makes use of.[23] The dream determines
its own horizons of experience and produces its own contents, without thereby permitting a categorical distinction
between empirical and transcendental moments. In a dream,
within the dream, *les mots* and *les choses* are in a fluid
sphere, as it were, with the other pairs of conceptual
thought: cause and effect, true and false. For the time being,
these conceptual pairs are all equal. Since the dream is an
instance that always creates things and their order anew, it
exercises a constitutive function sui generis that, however,

exists apart from the truth and the validity problematic. For there, within the dream, context and ground, the things and their order, represent only provisional moments of a categorically homogenous stream of representations.

Foucault illustrates the meaning of the imaginary in his dream conception by contrasting "image" and "imagination." While the image, as visual memory, replaces reality with crystallized representations, thereby portraying something parasitically dependent on the reality perceived in the waking hours, imagination is a deeper moment of creative experience that is superior to perception: "the image is not given at the culminating moment of imagination, but at the moment of its alteration. . . . To have an image is therefore to leave off imagining."[24] Here as well the similarity to Bachelard's obstacle problematic is surprising. At the same time, however, that aspect must be pointed out that most clearly distances Foucault from Bachelard. Namely, Foucault takes leave of the features of Bachelard's theory that have a strong psychological tone and tries to open up the imaginary, which Bachelard still conceived in terms of a philosophy of the subject, as an object domain accessible to a differentiated analysis. This intention should have been carried out in his promised "Anthropology of Expression." This region, which is defined by its subjectless production of the contents of the imaginary and which precedes and must inevitably produce all differences, should be observable in all the facets of its becoming.

> Expression is language, work of art, the ethical; here lurk all problems of style, all historical moments whose objective becoming is constitutive of that world whose directional meanings for our existence are exhibited by the dream.[25]

Problems of style are not just of concern to the promised, but undelivered, "Anthropology of Expression." Rather, they are also of concern for Foucault's other works which, in this respect, can be viewed as a realization of the "Anthropology of Expression."[26]

"Style" can designate many things: a person's immediate attitude which determines whether or not he or she is considered mad; the symptom-oriented practice of the modern doctor; or the interpretive attitude of the psychoanalyst or of Christian morality. On the basis of this quotation, it can already be conjectured that the object domain in need of explanation, which Foucault repeatedly tries to circumscribe with the terms *"episteme," "discourse,"* and "power," results from his unreflective postulation that all cultural phenomena belong to the expressive sphere, where neither claims of truth nor of rightness are appropriate.[27] On this level it is a matter of problems of style, that is, problems that are inaccessible even to an aesthetic critique[28] because a constitutive function is attributed to them. In other words, Foucault reduces cultural phenomena to a constitutive occurrence that is confined to the expressive sphere and that serves the same function as the subject.

To be sure, Foucault's first publication should not be taken too literally. Its arguments are still too unclear and its intention is still too vague. In his later years Foucault himself rarely referred to it, and it is perhaps not insignificant that this work was not more widely disseminated by means of translation into other languages. Apparently, when Foucault returned to this essay, he could not discover his own voice in its theses. Hubert Dreyfus and Paul Rabinow have pointed to the similarities between this work and themes in Heidegger,[29] and Bernhard Waldenfels[30] has made us aware that this publication, as well as those concerned with psychology and mental illness, are still strongly influenced by phenomenology, from which Foucault later distanced himself.[31] Focusing on the Bachelardian aspects of this work rather than pursuing other possible interpretations has the advantage of rendering prominent those epistemological themes which, I wish to show, run throughout Foucault's entire corpus.[32]

By way of summary, I would like to note those aspects of Foucault's early approach that can be understood as further developing Bachelard's philosophy.

1. The dream analysis and the program of an anthropology of expression are ostensibly discussed with the intent of criticizing knowledge. The tradition of dream analysis that Foucault takes up radically questions the subject-object problematic. The anonymous, creative character of the dream's imaginary stream makes fluid any possible determination of subject and object within the imaginary events. As a result, the precondition necessary for founding autonomous subjectivity falls away. Under such circumstances, the foundation problematic, conceived of as a conception of truth based on subjective or objective substance, loses its object as well.

2. Foucault's dream analysis is also characterized by a kind of epistemological break from the experience of the life-world.[33] Life is not seen here as the source of all cultural determinations, as is the case in the classic versions of the genetic fallacy. Rather, the true dimension of freedom, of being human, and of the fate of humanity take form in the dream, in the imaginative power of the imaginary.

3. The Foucauldian imaginary is ostensibly a creative moment, as is the case with Bachelard. The dream functions as the *creatio continua* of all dimensions of human existence.

The Dream, Madness, and the Critique of Psychology

Madness, the subject of Foucault's first major investigations, is related to the dream in many respects. Both exhibit a disquieting moment when compared to conscious thought. In addition, a prophetic dimension, the hint of absolute freedom, is attributed to them both. In the tradition that begins with German Romanticism, these topoi already turned the dream and madness into an almost homogenous complex, one which Foucault encounters in the history of culture. But the fact that the dream and madness are both objects of psychological inquiry is the connecting link that places them, in Foucault's particular perspective, on a theoretical continuum and allows their systematic status, in certain respects, to seem to be equivalent. In 1954, long before the appearance of *Madness and Civilization*,[34] the first of Foucault's works to deal with a critique of reason, the foreword to Binswanger's *Le rêve et l'existence* and the study *Mental Illness and Psychology*[35] emerged from the dream and the madness perspectives, respectively, and converged in a critique of psychology that shared a common structure. Viewed genetically, Foucault's later critique of the human sciences is a generalization of his epistemological critique of psychology.

If one accepts Foucault's intuition that the dream and madness act like sensors of a deep cultural region, upon which both psychology and its conceptual apparatus are dependent without being able to influence it in return, then psychology's task must seem to be unrealizable in principle.

[I]n wishing to carry out a psychology of madness, one is demanding that psychology should undermine its own conditions, that it should turn back to that which made it possible, and that it should circumvent what is for it, by definition, the unsupersedable. Psychology can never tell the truth about madness because it is madness that holds the truth of psychology.[36]

Foucault's argumentation is based on the conviction that psychology's standards of truth take on the obfuscatory function of an epistemological obstacle, as it were. This obfuscation is a result of the fact that psychology limits its understanding of madness or the dream experience to narrow features of truth that systematically block access to the broad epistemological significance of the dream or of madness, understood as a cultural complex. Just as the dream is no mere phantasmagoria of images, neither is madness a natural phenomenon. The false attribution of immediacy to the object turns the knowledge of the object into a false knowledge.

An ambiguity can already be noted in Foucault's first publications, which is repeated in an even more pronounced form in *Madness and Civilization*. In his first essay, Foucault announces an anthropology of expression that will use dream analysis to represent all aspects of the dream experience. The ambivalence consists in conceiving the dream as accessible to structural analysis, while at the same time thinking of it in the form of an experience. The same holds true for the madness problematic. In *Mental Illness and Psychology* Foucault writes:

> In fact, it is only in history that one can discover the sole concrete apriori from which mental illness draws, with the empty opening up of its possibility, its necessary figures.[37]

At another point Foucault expresses the hope for man that "one day, perhaps, he will be able to be free of all psychology and be ready for the tragic confrontation with madness."[38] Foucault vacillates in defining his theory's object domain. It is a matter of unambiguously determining the historically variable, pre-categorical level out of which the symbolic contents of our world are constituted. Naming such a level dream, madness, or irrationality does not essentially change the available options which, in Foucault's thought, are represented by a tension between Bataille's influence[39] on the one hand and Lévi-Strauss's[40] on the other. The domain of the dream or of madness can be presented either as a non-conceptualizable "other," and thus the encounter with it can only be indicated by an imprecise word like "experience," or it can be presented as a region accessible to a structuralist depth analysis whereby this region represents the conditions of possibility for all cultural phenomena. Foucault vacillates between these two options up to and including *Madness and Civilization*, even though it is difficult to make the two compatible in one theory. The tension between Bataille and Lévi-Strauss becomes understandable, and even demonstrates a certain complementarity between the two, however, when they are traced back to the endeavor to recast the romantic motif of an imaginary, pre-individualistic subjectivity into a post-metaphysical form. This ambivalence will first disappear when Foucault provides the second option, the structuralist analysis of the conditions for our culture, with the appropriate conceptual apparatus, that is, when it is freed from the remaining influences of a philosophy of the subject. This occurs in *The Order of Things*, where his analysis, by taking up the concept of *episteme*, enters upon a predominantly structuralist path that puts aside the figure of thought of an "other" of reason along with its corresponding aporetic thematization of experiences that transgress their given boundaries.

The Critique of the Human Sciences

Despite his later self-critique and change of topic, *The Order of Things* is still one of Foucault's most important writings because here the suppositions central to his reflection achieve a clear and universal form that is unsurpassed by his later work.

Foucault criticizes the history of culture as the history of invariant concepts that are thought to be defined, or definable, once and for all. Thus the human sciences, which are the subject matter of this book, are not defined as being concerned with a "person" who has stayed essentially the same throughout the course of history. Rather, it is claimed that the human sciences constitute the person on the basis of a historically conditioned cultural constellation that, by excluding other possible options, turns the person into the self-evident cultural figure of our time.

What gives this book a key position in Foucault's thought is the fact that the critique of self-referentiality[41] which, at least on the implicit level, is central to all his studies, is systematically and explicitly carried out here. Foucault takes this critique of self-referentiality as the starting point for a more comprehensive critique that should expose the aporias inherent in the basic contours of a philosophy of consciousness, which for Foucault means—without further qualification—the culture of modernity.

The course of argumentation found in the critique of self-reference is illuminating. Religious thought had sanctioned for humanity the impossibility of relating its finitude to an unfathomable, infinite principle that nonetheless founded the Order of Things. With the downfall of religious thought, the modern person emerged fully conscious of his or her finitude and was confronted with the task of seeking a stand-in for God's foundational role. For Foucault the drama of the modern person is the aporia of the foundation problematic. As such, its line of questioning already represents an irresolvable problem. Since the person is conscious of being thrown into a pregiven world of symbolic life and work relations that constitute him or her, the limits of his or her situation are known. But a consciousness constituted in this manner harbors within itself the impulse to investigate the spheres that condition it. Due to human finitude this infinite task is unrealizable in principle, and yet it still cannot be renounced; it sentences the person to repeatedly take on this challenge and to try to overcome the limits that repeatedly arise.

Foucault describes in detail the endless vacillation of the modern human sciences. From the narrow perspective of their empirical approach they try to discern their constitutive preconditions, thereby forming the doubling of the person into the empirical and transcendental moments that characterize modernity.[42] The essence of the question runs as follows: How can truths gained by empirical knowledge attain the status of conditions of possibility for these very same truths? This key question brings an epistemological form of argumentation into play: The truth of the human sciences is a truth "that is of the same order as the object."[43] It is a matter of a truth that the human sciences must arrive at by analyzing the objects of life, work, and language themselves, such that the knowledge of such object-constituting domains must finally find itself burdened with the weight of naive realism or positivism, in any case with a completely precritical process. Because the human sciences do not constitute their object domain but rather proceed from it as an unproblematically presupposed given, in the final analysis they merely represent a variation on the realism of traditional epistemology, and their object, whose essential characteristics they endlessly research, turns out to be what Bachelard would, without hesitation, call an epistemological obstacle. Foucault claims that the structure of the different knowledge domains is erected on these fragile presuppositions. On their basis philosophical reflection investigates the essential features of being human.

> And so we find philosophy falling asleep once more in the hollow of this Fold; this time not the sleep of Dogmatism, but that of Anthropology. All empirical knowledge, provided it concerns man, can serve as a possible philosophical field in which the foundation of knowledge, the definition of its limits, and, in the end, the truth of all truth must be discoverable. The anthropological configuration of modern philosophy consists in doubling over dogmatism, in dividing it into two different levels each lending support to and limiting the other: the precritical analysis of what man is in his *essence* becomes the analytic of everything that can, in general, be presented to man's experience.[44]

Foucault conceived the critique of the human sciences as the aporia of a modernity characterized by the motif of self-relation. Foucault is able to repeat the epistemological critique of realism with the "person" of the human sciences, because the person, by virtue of his or her self-relation, turns itself into an object, thereby internalizing the knowledge problematic, as it were, and reproducing all the difficulties of traditional epistemology. If Foucault's critique of the human sciences can be construed in this way, then it attains the status of an epochal turning point that liberates the human sciences from the sterility of the traditional epistemological search for the true human substance, and that acknowledges the human sciences as offering their counterpart to the natural sciences by heralding a still ill-defined form of anti-science.

In this form, however, Foucault's critique has the ultimately misleading effect of proposing a convincing thesis that, nevertheless, addresses the wrong problem. What Foucault misunderstands is that the human sciences and the basic self-referential construction of the philosophy of consciousness are not the same. Habermas has shown that Foucault's critique of the human sciences can indeed be attributed to the paradigm of a philosophy of consciousness, but not to the human sciences nor to the culture of modernity. He argues that by referring to a symbolically prestructured reality the human sciences, as reconstructive sciences that proceed on the basis of the participant perspective,[45] suggest how the aporias Foucault analyzed can be avoided by drawing on analytic philosophy's solution to the philosophy of consciousness.[46] Foucault, however, is too strongly influenced by an epistemological problematic derived from the natural sciences; he is able to advance his line of argumentation because his method attributes an observer perspective to the human sciences that allows them to be characterized as more or less positivist. This train of thought can be pursued and the path of an archaeological anti-science can be entered upon only when the positivist reduction of the human sciences can be derived from the epistemological problematic. For that to occur, Foucault must pay the price. It must be a matter of an anti-science that despite all indeterminacy can prescribe at least one *ex negativo* point: It must ignore the problem of its own foundations because this discussion would result in a relapse into the problematic faced by traditional epistemology or rather by prescientific realism, that is, the problematic of pure substance.

Anti-Science

Foucault suffers from an epistemological misunderstanding of the history of culture. The difference between the empirical sciences, which investigate the regularities of nature, and the human sciences, which reconstruct the rules of a symbolically prestructured world, escapes him. Instead he favors a quasi-mathematical, scientific attitude which now, with the aid of structuralist measures, should also prove successful in the domain of the history of culture as well. But for Foucault the critique of the human sciences is not merely the critical means whereby the basic contours of the culture of modernity can be rejected as aporetic. The critique of the human sciences, when interpreted as an epistemological critique of knowledge at its very core, lacks an episodic character. Rather, it represents a development of the critical model already applied in the earlier studies of the dream, madness, and the clinical gaze. Now an "anti-science" will confront the foundationalist wake left behind by a closed, self-referential knowing which will be able to escape the latter's "anthropological sleep."

The Order of Things offers no comprehensive definition of what an anti-science should be. Foucault adopts a feature common both to the psychoanalysis found in Freud's metapsychological writings and to ethnology. Neither is concerned with the person in itself as an anthropologically pregiven object, but rather each researches the anonymous, historical field of its emergence:

> their development has one particular feature, which is that, despite their quasi-universal "bearing," they never, for all that, come near to a general concept of man: at no moment do they come near to isolating a quality in him that is specific, irreducible, and uniformly valid wherever he is given to experience. The idea of a "psychoanalytic anthropology," and the idea of a "human nature" reconstituted by ethnology, are no more than pious wishes. Not only are they able to do without the concept of man, they are also unable to pass through it, for they always address themselves to that which constitutes his outer limits.[47]

Whereas psychoanalysis and ethnology primarily provide examples that show where the line runs between the anti-sciences and the human sciences, in addition to showing how some limited domains of the person-constituting region can be described, linguistics best illustrates the features that an anti-science should exhibit. Linguistics constitutes its object;

> it is therefore not a theoretical reworking of knowledge acquired elsewhere, the interpretation of an already accomplished reading of phenomena; it does not offer a "linguistic version" of the facts observed in the human sciences, it is rather the principle of a primary decipherment: to a gaze forearmed by linguistics, things attain to existence only in so far as they are able to form the elements of a signifying system.[48]

So far Foucault seems to have found the human sciences' counterpart to the constitutive achievements of theory formation in the natural sciences in an anti-science oriented on linguistics. Even further: Linguistics allows the separation between mathematics and the human sciences to be overcome. Thus

> we find that by means of this emergence of structure (as an invariable relation within a totality of elements) the relation of the human sciences to mathematics has been opened up once more, and in a wholly new dimension. . . .[49]

In closing, Foucault asks himself "what language must be in order to structure in this way what is nevertheless not in itself either word or discourse, and in order to articulate itself on the pure forms of knowledge."[50] With this question he refers to the difficult and important problem of how to develop an anti-science that will offer a convincing alternative to the transcendental subject. It is a matter of "purifying the old empirical reason by constituting formal languages, and of applying a second critique of pure reason on the basis of new forms of the mathematical *a priori*."[51] An anti-science constituted in such a manner must be able to liberate the historical event from the false compulsion towards continuity found in the humanistic writing of history, which conceals its breaks and discontinuities behind the reassuring idea that humanity remains self-identical throughout its development. Given Foucault's premises, the idea of a human history or of a "history of the self," that is, a history of the variations on one and the same human essence, must seem as implausible as something like the history of the atom from Democritus to today. What would be lacking in such an account would be the transformations of the relations—in Foucault's words, the *episteme*—whose structural features, according to Foucault, represent the frame, the historical a priori, of cultural life relations. Cultural objects are always misunderstood when viewed outside the constitutive web of *episteme*, because their identity can only exist in a situated manner within the epistemic constellation to which they belong.

Foucault does not provide a comprehensive definition of what he calls "*episteme*." *Episteme* should designate a positive order, a middle region that lies between the "codified gaze" of lifeworld experience and "reflective knowledge"; it should fulfill the function of articulating each level on its own and in relation with the other. Like the concepts dream, madness, and the clinical gaze, *episteme* seems to be a provisional term for a historical a priori the contours of which are not yet clear. Seen functionally it is an occurrence, like Bachelard's creative spirit, that is characterized by the following: It produces its own objects, is disassociated from lifeworld relations, and is itself historically variable, that is, it cannot be traced back to clearly identifiable structural features. This holds true, to my mind, despite the restrictions made necessary by the strong structuralist tendencies found in *The Order of Things*. If the historical a priori was still ambivalent in the dream analysis and in *Madness and Civilization*, where it was conceptualized both as experience (following Bataille) and also as structure, then in *The Order of Things* Foucault's thought achieves its clearest scientific, if not scientistic, turn.

Indeed, the use of linguistics as the model for characterizing anti-science seems to drive Foucault's position very close to a structuralist method. To be sure, such a method would renounce transhistorical regularities but, nonetheless, by using the concept of *episteme* it should make possible the anonymous, historical conditions of possibility for knowledge, thereby providing a comprehensive definition for an entire epoch by relying on structural features. This claim will soon be retracted, however. Already in *The Archaeology of Knowledge*, where the idea of an autonomous signifying system that determines the historical process has not yet been relinquished, Foucault writes in an implicitly self-critical manner:

> my aim is most decidedly not to use the categories of cultural totalities (whether world-views, ideal types, the particular spirit of an age) in order to impose on history, despite itself, the forms of structural analysis.[52]

The imprecise methodological arrangement of the theses advanced in *The Order of Things* forces Foucault into a position the difficulties of which he is well aware. First among these difficulties is that of an anti-science oriented on linguistics, which should describe the abrupt transformations of a totalizing *episteme* and yet stumbles on structuralism's traditional weakness—namely, its inability to take historical becoming into account. Foucault's emphatic references to historical breaks, to history's kaleidoscopic revolutionization in the succession of the three *epistemes* of the Renaissance, the classical period, and modernity, are paradoxical in a book like *The Order of Things*, in which the implicit claim to non-ideologically and directly describe what "really" happened can constantly be felt. It is, after all, precisely the occurrence that must become the object of analysis. Instead, Foucault can only take note of the sudden rise and fall of various *epistemes* without giving the slightest indication of which forms of power led to these historical discontinuities.

Chapter Three

The Archaeology

The Archaeology of Knowledge is presented as a more methodologically precise version of Foucault's earlier material investigations. Yet it clearly departs from the structuralist motifs that were to be found in *The Birth of the Clinic* and *The Order of Things*. This work is of particular relevance to my concerns because it clearly illustrates that Foucault, in order to be able to draw a line between himself and a structuralism that avoids falling into the subjectivism or humanism he criticizes, must increasingly rely on Bachelard's epistemological problematic.

Because Foucault cannot plausibly explain the sudden mutations of an *episteme* that comprehends all the appearances of an epoch, he introduces two essential correctives to his theory with his archaeological analysis of discourse. Due to theoretical constraints analogous to those that caused Kuhn to change his conception of scientific revolutions from one that emphasized a succession of paradigms to one that focused on a multitude of micro-revolutions (which considerably weakened his initial paradigm),[1] Foucault must switch from the concept of *episteme* to that of discourse.[2] Specifically, he must conceptualize a way of writing history that neither resorts to the continuity of the humanistic writing of history nor to structural constants, that avoids the puzzling breaks that are associated with the concept of *episteme* and yet does not relinquish *episteme's* systematic status as the historical a priori.

The major periodizations of his material analyses remain constant even after this turn in his thought. His conceptualization of historical events, however, now emerges from the precarious interaction of several overlapping "regional" discourses, none of which alone possesses the key to an epoch. His theory's claim to totality is relinquished. The second corrective in the transition from *episteme* to discourses consists in the fact that discourses, unlike *episteme*, are thought in a necessary relation to practices,[3] even though they are autonomous in the final analysis. This smooths the way to the later theory of power.

The unchanged anti-humanistic tone of Foucault's theory becomes obvious in the first pages of *The Archaeology of Knowledge* with the striking distinction between documents and monuments. The science of archaeology should abandon the hermeneutic attitude which sees in the traces of the past fragments of meaning requiring interpretation. The point here is not to "interpret" the document ". . . [to] attempt to decide whether it is telling the truth or what . . . its expressive value [is]."[4] What is essential is first of all to view the historical material, apart from all hermeneutics, in a purely descriptive manner—as a monument which, in its external silence, can be sorted, ordered, and put in relation but cannot be "interpreted." With his critique of the document Foucault repeats the main argument of his critical epistemology, which he continually reformulates with many inventive variations. The chapter on the aporias of the human sciences, the critique of epistemology for presupposing commentary found in the foreword to *The Birth of the Clinic*, the brilliant critique of Platonism found in the foreword to Deleuze's *Différence et répétition*,[5] as well as other passages, could all be cited in support of the basic thesis that every search for a primordial substance of things, or for a primordial identity of subjects, is subject to the fallacy of conceptualizing truth as the purity of the object.[6] The pursuit of epistemological purity, which seeks the pure truth and consequently becomes hopelessly enmeshed in aporetic doublings, belongs to the documentary writing of history. The archaeologist, by contrast, works in an unstructured field of elements which can be combined only in accordance with their possible relations.

The choice of the word "archaeology" to designate Foucault's method is undoubtedly successful. True, it can easily be shown that the archaeologist is also unable to manage without a hermeneutic preunderstanding of lifeworld relations. To be sure, such an objection could be raised with regard to almost every page of Foucault's work; it touches on a principal weakness of his theory as a whole and would suffice for an external critique. Yet such a critique would be sterile, in a certain sense, because it does not have to enter into the substance of his thought. If the intent, however, is to pursue Foucault's motifs internally, then the concept of archaelogy best conveys the status that Foucault would like to confer on his theory.

Following my discussion of the critique of the human sciences, I argued that in order to be able to formulate his epistemological critique of the transcendental-anthropological doubling of the person Foucault had to ignore the distinctive aspects of the human sciences' object domain, which is linguistically prestructured, and assimilate it to the object domain of the natural sciences. Since the tools for his epistemological critique stem from Bachelard's treatment of the natural sciences, in order to employ the corresponding epistemological concepts the history of culture must first be assimilated to the history of science. Archaeology's preoccupation with the "objectified," silenced, and quasi-naturalized remnants of human cultures serves this end. For all that, it is not only a matter of explicating the positivist project of contemplating and describing the main features of one's own culture from the observer perspective. Rather, this describing comes about by means of the archaeologist's active and constructive intervention in his or her raw material. Foucault defines archaeology as "a discipline devoted to silent monuments, inert traces, objects without context."[7] The task of the archaeologist does not consist in seeking the truth of fragmentary objects within themselves, however, but in creating a context for them in which they can each find their place.

In *The Order of Things* Foucault conceptualized *episteme* as a middle region that lies between the formalized sciences and everyday experience. In the *Archaeology* and in some minor writings[8] the epistemological function of this region, now renamed "discourse" or "knowledge," is clarified. Discourses only appear in the plural; they comprise only certain aspects of an analysis of culture; and they are tied to social practices, a sphere that will enter into the foreground in his later writings on power. Now as ever, the analysis of discourse pays heed to the "breaks," to the discontinuities and schisms in historical development. But here it is not a matter of the sudden ascents and declines of an all-embracing *episteme*, the sequence of which was so implausible. The picture becomes more fluid; the epochal revolutions are replaced by a multitude of smaller discontinuities that are to be analyzed on the micrological level. The epistemological coherence of larger time spans is replaced by the precarious balance of unstable micro-struggles that permeate and ultimately constitute the discourse. The outlines of the micrological analysis can already be found in the *Archaeology*, even though it is not yet fully developed, as it will be in the theory of power.

In the following I will examine the structure of the *Archaeology* by way of the three Bachelardian motifs that I have chosen as my interpretive framework—that is, by way of the critique of knowledge (sections 10 and 11), creative subjectivity (section 12), and the epistemological break (section 13).

The Disintegration of Immediacy

The Archaeology of Knowledge is a single, detailed attempt to expose the unity and immediacy of objects or concepts as false or, in other words, as epistemological obstacles. If the act of defining can be characterized as the description of an object's substantial attributes, then archaeology pleads for the impossibility of defining. Not only the introductory *pars destruens*, in which every remnant of the humanistic-hermeneutic tradition of historical writing is supposed to be cleared away, but also the *pars construens* stands under the banner of this Bachelardian model of an epistemological critique of knowledge. The laborious construction of the archaeological terminology is made possible by dissolving every form of immediacy into relation. I will provide a rough sketch of Foucault's procedure.

After the historical form of cultural humanism was radically deconstructed (*entstrukturiert*) and banned from the field of analysis in the name of a critique of "continuity," an "immense region" was made accessible to Foucault's analysis which he tentatively defined as the entirety of statements. The concept of the "statement" initiates a long chain of tentative definitions along with the displacement of this defining onto additional concepts in need of definition. Accordingly, the statement is first of all "an event that neither the language (*langue*) nor the meaning can exhaust."[9] If the archaeological approach makes the negative delimitations of the statement vis-à-vis structuralism and hermeneutics readily apparent, not much has yet been gained by considering statements as events. That is, events only form the "material with which one is dealing . . . in its raw, neutral state"[10] and this in a context that Foucault names "discourse." This formulation remains hopelessly vague; the only thing it clarifies is that statements, in being thought of as events, are not subject to the fallacy of substantialism. The pair discourse/enunciative event, although related to the pair structure/event, should not be understood structurally, according to Foucault.[11] It is not a matter of investigating a limited number of rules that make an unlimited number of applications possible, as is the case in the analysis of language. Rather, it is a matter of an immense, but in principle limited, complex of actually formulated statements. The focus, then, is not on the conditions of possibility of statements but on the conditions of their existence.[12]

Recourse to this distinction, however, hardly contributes to developing a more adequate understanding of what a statement is. It is still the case that a determination of the statement must be able to indicate how it differentiates itself from other linguistic concepts, how by asserting its externality it can disregard subjective intentions of meaning, and above all, what distinguishes it from arbitrary "meaningless" combinations of signs. In the interim, however, Foucault stands by his first provisional definition and proceeds by describing the relations between statements. What is surprising here is not only that the author builds his theory on a conception of the statement about which nothing definite can be said as yet, but also that what is announced as a description of the relations between statements[13] is ultimately carried out as an analysis of the possible contexts of statements.[14] It will be shown later that a fusion of context and system of rules is presupposed thereby which does not simply indicate an unintended lack of clarity in the presentation. Rather, this fusion, seen systematically, is central to the *Archaeology* and constitutes one of its fundamental weaknesses.[15]

Foucault investigates four areas to which statements can refer. Statements can refer to an object,[16] a form of syntactical structuring,[17] a coherent and permanent semantic dimension of concepts,[18] and to a thematic continuity.[19] These groupings, which are "discovered," so to speak, and which correspond to Foucault's material investigations to a large extent,[20] can be criticized on the basis of the familiar epistemological tenet derived from Bachelard which runs as follows. Objects, syntactic types, semantic elements, and thematic strategies do not, in themselves, constitute unities to which statements can refer. They do not conceal within them their own inherent substance, their own inherent truth, a core that awaits "discovery." Instead, Foucault's deconstruction shows that a network of heterogeneous relations lies hidden behind apparent monolithic unities, such as the unities of psychiatric or clinical discourse. These relations render prominent discontinuities rather than continuities, and dispersions or dispersals rather than unities. The task of the archaeologist consists in conceptualizing discontinuities and dispersals as a rule-guided system.

> Hence the idea of describing these dispersions themselves; of discovering whether, between these elements, which are certainly not organized as a progressively deductive structure, nor as an enormous book that is being gradually and continuously written, nor as the oeuvre of a collective subject, one cannot discern a regularity.[21]

On the basis of this hypothesis, which guided Foucault's material investigations and is now formulated more generally, Foucault should be able to replace conventional disciplinary or conceptual unities with new complexes. These complexes, which are marked by a system of dispersions, are called "discourses." Discourses are the actual object of archaeology. They constitute unities sui generis out of statements which, even in their dispersal, are subject to particular rules of formation specific to each case. A statement can only be recognized as such within the structuring function that applies rules of formation as a constitutive moment of a discourse.

By adding discourse and rules of formation to the statement, the basic concepts that form the conceptual framework of the *Archaeology* have been introduced. The entire construction of archeological theory relies on these concepts and on their reciprocal relation.

Statement, Discourse, Rules of Formation

Although statements are introduced at the beginning of *The Archaeology of Knowledge* as the elementary units of discourse, in the course of Foucault's complicated account they attain a new status. The statement comes to be defined as a function that determines the modalities of the sign's existence. To some degree Foucault is forced into this change of definition. If he had insisted on his initial, propaedeutic definition of the statement as a unit, he would have had to accept epistemological implications that are irreconcilable with his approach.

> Far from being the principle of individualization of groups of "signifiers" (the meaningful "atom," the minimum on the basis of which there is meaning), the statement is that which situates these meaningful units in a space in which they breed and multiply.[22]

If it were understood as a substantial unit, the statement would be an example of the naive realism that is criticized in Bachelard's epistemology. It would be an object with, so to speak, a false foundation: An object whose truth rested in itself. Thus, in being made more precise, this definition is brought closer to Bachelard. The question is no longer one of the statement, but of the enunciative function, which is a relation. By referring to its discursive context, the enunciative function designates the sign's mode of existence. Function also determines a sign's meaning within a structured context. In the sentence "The golden mountain is in California," for example, the raw material provided by the sign first becomes a statement when it is related to a literary context.

This, however, does not eliminate the problems that arise from the intentional dimension of each statement.[23] On the level of application, context alone is insufficient to exhaust the meaning of a statement, since for that to be the case one would have to be able to presuppose a context that also takes into account the illocutionary force of a statement considered as an *expression*[24] in the sense of speech act theory.

One could try to make Foucault's conception of the enunciative function plausible by comparing it to mathematics. In a certain sense mathematical symbols are first meaningful when a mathematical context attributes a determinate existence to them which allows them to appear as formulas, theorems, or equations.[25] To be sure, in the case of the enunciative function it would be a matter of an improbable mathematics without mathematicians. But even if such a solution were practicable, the problem of the definition of the statement would be displaced onto that of the definition of discourses or of discursive formations and rules of formation. The latter, in acting as the structuring context, would have to carry the entire burden of theory construction.

On the one hand, discursive formations are the conditions for the existence of statements. That is, they are the occurrences that alone form the context in which the enunciative functions can be given. On the other hand, when it comes to defining discursive formations via the type of regularity, that is, the "rules of formation" that in some way structure them as "systems of dispersion,"[26] Foucault replies that discursive formations are groups of statements. This answer ensnares the whole argument in a tangle of mutual reproofs.

> It can be said that the mapping of discursive formations, independently of other principles of possible unification, reveals the specific level of the statement; but it can also be said that the description of statements and of the way in which the enunciative level is organized leads to the individualization of the discursive formations. The two approaches are equally justifiable and reversible. The analysis of the statement and that of the formation are established correlatively. When the time finally comes to found a theory, it will have to define a deductive order.[27]

Such a predicament must be unsatisfactory to a work that was supposed to provide the methodological framework for Foucault's theory. The actual difficulty, however, is not that the grounding of the theory is suspended until a later point in time. Rather, it lies in the uncertain status that the rules of formation enjoy in theory construction. Strictly speaking these rules, due to their constitutive function, would have to represent the key role, the true secret of archaeology. And in fact they are characterized as the conditions under which discursive formations are structured. "The conditions to which the elements of this division . . . are subject we shall call the rules of formation."[28] Foucault cannot say what these conditions are, however, because the archaeological method does not allow for their systematic definition. Admittedly, he conceptualizes discourse analysis in terms of a theory of constitution, but his insistence on the conditions for the existence of statements suggests that he must simultaneously renounce the categorical distinction between empirical and transcendental moments since such a distinction would mean that his theory had relapsed into the aporetic doubling for which *The Order of Things* criticized the human sciences. For this reason he arrives at a paradoxical formulation of discursive formation. Although it only consists of categorically homogenous statements, as we have just seen, the totality of its statements nevertheless functions as a complex of rules of formation which are conditions for the existence of just that discursive formation. As a result, ultimately no analytic distinction can be made between statements, discursive formations, and rules of formation. Foucault expresses himself in the following manner:

> A statement belongs to a discursive formation as a sentence belongs to a text, and a proposition to a deductive whole. But whereas the regularity of a sentence is defined by the laws of a language (*langue*), and that of a proposition by the laws of logic, the regularity of statements is defined by the discursive formation itself. The fact of its belonging to a discursive formation and the laws that govern it are one and the same thing.[29]

The assimilation of context and rule and the blending of the empirical level with that of validity rule out any possible systematization. Even the indication that discourse formations are not concerned with principles but rather with "actual dispersals" does not do much to change the difficulties mentioned above because in this case it must be explained how an actual dispersal (an event) can obtain the status of a lawlike regularity. Thus, Foucault's baroque description leaves one important question unanswered. Namely, how can differences, which could transform the gray surface of signs into meaningful relations among statements, emerge from a categorically neutral and purely external field—from an area, that is, from which intentional aims and reflexivity are banished?

The Semiologization of the Imaginary

Since no coherent line of argumentation can be recognized in the structure of the *Archaeology*, it seems easier to seek Foucault's intention in the Bachelardian line of questioning. In the two earlier sections I frequently referred to the first of three Bachelardian motifs that leaves its stamp on the *Archaeology:* Namely, the systematic critique of the traditional epistemological line of questioning. One can now continue with a second motif which renders Foucault's complicated construction, if not more coherent, at least more comprehensible. The confusing exchange regarding the definitions of statements and of discourse, along with the depiction of a semiological becoming in which particular elements, contexts, and regulatory instances are a priori categorically indifferentiable and yet possess the ability to articulate themselves in ever new constellations and dispersals, suggest a comparison with Foucault's early works.

Faint traces of Foucault's early conception of the dream can be recognized under the features of the archaeological analysis of discourse. The conceptual apparatus of semiology loses its puzzling character and appears as one coherent, if unsuccessful, attempt at theory formation when it is postulated that the intention that was announced programmatically in the 1954 foreword, that is, the immature formulation of an anthropology of expression, lies behind these awkward structures of argumentation.

The motifs of an autonomously formed imaginary production in which subject and object, elements of a context and their rules, constantly vary without thereby surrendering their fundamental homogeneity, are in fact preserved in the wrappings of an analysis of discourse. These motifs do not refer so much to Lévi-Strauss's "unconscious activity of the mind"[30] whose universal laws were, from the very start, irreconcilable with Foucault's relativistic conception of history. Rather, it seems that Bachelard's conception of spirit as a lively creativity that cannot be reduced to any structures is echoed here. This thesis can elucidate both the philosophical intention behind Foucault's methodological efforts as well as the grounds for its failure. For, based on this hypothesis, the *Archaeology* seems to be an attempt to transcribe, with the assistance of semiology, the philosophical intuition of the creative imaginary into a scientific or, better said, "anti-scientific," form.

In the *Archaeology* the romantic motifs of Bachelard and of Foucault's early writing converge with the structuralist influences at work in *The Order of Things* and *The Birth of the Clinic* in an attempt at synthesis that raises methodological claims as a kind of *semiologization of the imaginary*. The confusion that arose from overburdening the semiological dimension with the creative character of the imaginary has already shown the difficulty of creating such a synthesis, however. Foucault is aware of this difficulty. Finding a way out of this unsuccessful synthesis requires a new orientation. Within the archaeological approach he could resolve the hybrid character of his construction either by favoring a pure analysis of signs or by returning to a conception of the imaginary consistent with the philosophy of consciousness. Both options are untenable for Foucault, however. A pure analysis of signs would deprive discourse of the quasi-performative attributes that support his philosophical idea of a historical a priori, while the return to the imaginary would contravene his anti-subjectivistic attitude. As a result of this dilemma, a change in course occurs which allows power to emerge from the "practices" that were still considered marginal in the *Archaeology*. As the new attempt at synthesis, power takes the place of the analysis of signs.

Before I turn to the theory of power, however, I would like to address the third Bachelardian motif that I have taken to frame my interpretation of the *Archaeology*: The problem of the epistemological break.

The Neutralization of the Validity Problematic

For Bachelard, the concept of the epistemological break between scientific construction and the images of everyday life was closely connected to the concept of scientific spirit. The question of how we make the transition from prejudice-laden perceptions to abstract knowledge was thought to be the domain of a special kind of psychoanalysis. Thus, on the one hand Foucault has to adopt the idea of the epistemological break because, in addition to addressing his theory's epistemological core, it forms one of the most important watersheds between his approach and that of phenomenology.

> What *The Archaeology of Knowledge* invalidates is . . . the general topic of "cognition." Cognition is the continuity of science and experience, the indissoluble complexity of both, their uncertain reversibility.[31]

On the other hand, if Bachelard is to be granted an anti-psychologistic reception, his conceptual scheme must be purified of every form of subjectivism. Foucault's position with regard to both demands is unmistakable.

> There is an illusion that consists of the supposition that science is grounded in the plenitude of a con-

> crete and lived experience. . . . But it is equally illu-
> sory to imagine that science is established by an act
> of rupture and decision.[32]

A conception of knowledge, understood as that "of which
one can speak in a discursive practice,"[33] lies between these
two options; it forms the connecting link that should formulate the epistemological break in a new, non-psycholog-
ical form. Archaeology takes the place of the creative act of
the scientist who construes theory as an abstractive achievement in the face of the images of everyday experience.
Through the means of discourse analysis, archaeology
should be able to disclose a historical middle region that
reinterprets the epistemological break from now on as the
achievement of a semiological articulation. The occurrence
of knowledge

> defines the laws of formation of scientific objects
> and therefore provides the links or the oppositions
> between science and experience. . . . Knowledge
> determines the space in which science and experi-
> ence part and are situated in relation to one
> another.[34]

Seen in this way, the objects of Foucault's material investigations, from madness to the clinic up through criminology,
now appear as so many examples of the mediating function
knowledge carries out between science and experience. This
function, however, also plays an important role with regard
to method, especially with regard to the validity problematic.

Foucault can afford to advocate a sovereign, well-bal-
anced position with regard to a problem area that is desig-
nated by the so-called "internalist" and "externalist"[35] lines
in the Anglo-Saxon tradition.

> *Epistemological* extrapolation should not be con-
> fused with the (always legitimate and possible) anal-
> ysis of the formal structures which may characterize
> a scientific discourse. But it suggests that these
> structures are enough to define for a science the his-

torical law of its appearance and unfolding. *Genetic extrapolation* should not be confused with the (always legitimate and possible) description of the context—whether discursive, technical, economic or institutional—in which a science appeared; but it suggests that the internal organization of a science and its formal norms can be described on the basis of its external conditions. In one case, the science is given the responsibility of explaining its own historicity; in the other, various historical determinations are required to explain a scientificity.[36]

Foucault's thesis possesses at least prima facie plausibility because its result, at least, seems to recognize and avoid the disadvantages of both one-sided approaches. Yet for all that, the strategy basically aims at neutralizing, not resolving, the problem.

This fundamental idea is by no means unique to Foucault; it appears in Bachelard's and Kuhn's[37] historical works on science as well. In both approaches, anonymous scientific structures (axioms or paradigms) are linked to reductive, psychological conceptions of the subject. Scientific structures become the only rationally accessible aspect of the history of science, while the activity of the scientist is neutralized to unproblematic quantities such as an "epistemological act" or a "change in form." They are turned into the "black box" of theory.

Foucault's program is similar to these other approaches, but its outcome is more radical. Discourse analysis is governed by the attempt, spurred on by a positivist impetus, not only to illuminate structures epistemologically, apart from all remnants of subjectivism, but also to illuminate the pair characteristic of this type of theory as a whole, structure/creativity, in the same manner. Hence, semiology is systematically overburdened; it is actually forced into taking on a pragmatic dimension.

Of course, discourses are composed of signs; but what they do is more than use these signs to desig-

nate things. It is this *more* that renders them irre-
ducible to the language (*langue*) and to speech. It is
this "*more*" that we must reveal and describe.[38]

Foucault's many formulations, such as "discursive practice," "discursive events," and "enunciative functions,"
denote multiple aspects of this attempt to fuse structural
and creative moments into one subjectless complex which,
nevertheless, should act as the functional equivalent for
subjective achievements. An important consequence follows from this project. Bachelard's pair construction/spirit
was still able to accommodate, to some degree, the role of
the scientist in his or her scrutinizing and justificatory functions. Foucault's more radical epistemological take on this
approach, however, leads to a complete marginalization of
rational argumentation, which becomes a superficial phenomenon, the froth in the stream of discourse. The changing configurations of discourse, like the images in a dream,
cannot be judged by the criteria of validity. They function
like sequences of an oneiric monologue, with the scientist
fruitlessly trying to ground validity claims on the basis of
their variable contents. If discourse and its constellation of
knowledge change, then the objects, with regard to which
arguments and truth claims are exchanged in any given his-
toric epoch, dissolve. Therewith, the core of the scientific
and cultural process is shifted, in the Foucauldian model,
from the level of problematizable validity claims raised by
rational subjects to that of the non-problematizable social
validity of a historically defined constellation of knowledge.
Scientific progress and the cognitive import of moral-practical processes of learning are reduced to mere *problems of
style* due to their dependence on unproblematizable knowledge claims. In order to make explicit the continuity in
Foucault's line of development in this regard, I will repeat a
quote from the 1954 foreword: "Expression is language,
work of art, the ethical; here lurk all problems of style, all
historical moments whose objective becoming is constitutive of the world."[39] As impressive as the attempt to neu-

tralize the validity problematic may seem, it does not achieve the form of an argument (and, of course, cannot achieve this form as a matter of principle). The "pure description of discursive events" denies the participation of the describer (better said, the interpreter) in the object under investigation. The performative contradiction of a theory that tries to undermine scientific argumentation could only be avoided by laying claim to an "other" of reason or by believing that one had attained a privileged "omnipotent perspective."

But Foucault the archaeologist rejects auratic formulations as well as irrational tendencies. In spite of everything, he understands himself as a scientist (even if it is with reference to an anti-science) and therefore comes to see the difficulties associated with the discourse-analytic approach.

The obfuscation of the validity problematic will continue to be a conspicuous weakness of Foucault's theory. After the period of *The Archaeology of Knowledge*, however, a less demanding strategy is pursued which implicitly concedes the failure of his analysis of discourse. Foucault relinquishes the idea of an autonomous system of signs along with all methodological programs.

With the transition to the theory of power, what could be called Foucault's "scientistic" period comes to an end. The problems that it addressed are, from now on, either ignored or redefined. As we shall see, however, the basic motifs that guided his work remain the same.

Chapter Four

The Theory of Power

The historical upheaval associated with the student revolts of 1968 was clearly among the factors that led Foucault to develop his theory of power. Without a doubt, Foucault and many other intellectuals of his generation were led to think about the mechanisms of a complex society by their firsthand experience with the multiple ways that the power structure was prepared to nearly seamlessly respond to the demands of the student movement. This new line of questioning was encouraged further when, at the beginning of the 1970s, the Marxists throughout Europe discovered a new interest in the specific functioning of the state and power apparatuses.

This new aspect of Foucault's thought, which is sketched out in "The Discourse on Language" and completed in *Discipline and Punish*, also lends itself, however, to an immanent reading; that is, it can be seen as an attempt to resolve the problems that remained unanswered by concluding his semiological period with *The Archaeology of*

Knowledge. Admittedly, the semiological period was the scientistic high point of Foucault's thought, but *The Archaeology of Knowledge* also introduced the element of practices, which already took power into account. Foucault writes that the statement enters

> various fields of use, is subjected to transferences or modifications, is integrated into operations and strategies in which its identity is maintained or effaced. Thus the statement circulates, is used, disappears, allows or prevents the realization of a desire, serves or resists various interests, participates in challenge and struggle, and becomes a theme of appropriation or rivalry.[1]

With the failure of his discourse analysis, understood as the description of an autonomous system of signs, power is raised from its ultimately marginal role in the field of the use of discourses to the actual center of his theory. As a result of this new position, the previous features of power must be redetermined and reorganized.

In this chapter as well, my interpretation will be guided by the three Bachelardian motifs that provided the basis earlier in this work for reconstructing the development of Foucault's thought up until the *Archaeology*. The basic thesis that is tied to this interpretation runs as follows: The special features of the theory of power as well as the definition of the concept of power itself can best be explained as resulting from a transposition of epistemological and scientific-historical arguments into a theory of society. Further, this kind of explanation allows many aspects of Foucault's theory of power to be seen as coherently advancing the approach of his earlier writings.

In the previous sections it was shown how Bachelard's model, with its contrast between the productivity of scientific constructions and the sterile substantialism of traditional epistemology, is repeated as a component part of all of Foucault's works up until *The Archaeology of Knowledge*. The psychological versus the romantic conception of the dream; psychiatry versus the experience of madness; the human sciences versus the anti-sciences, which are oriented on the concept of *episteme*; and the hermeneutic understanding of meaning versus the archaeological analysis of discourse. All these unpredictable oppositions can be traced back to the topos of a critique of realism that spurns the naive search for a truth hidden in the essence of the object (or subject) as mistaken. A similar opposition can be found in Foucault's theory of power as well. It is reflected in the contrast between what can be provisionally termed a substantialist and an ontological formulation of the concept of power.

The Dualism within Power

One does not have to force Foucault's wording all that much to maintain that there is a distinction between two different forms of power. In "The Discourse on Language,"[2] which serves as a kind of transition from the semiological studies to those on the theory of power in the 1970s, the doubled articulation of the concept of power emerges with respect to the historical problematization of the concept of truth. Foucault distinguishes between the *"will to knowledge,"* which characterizes the dominant form of power since Plato, and a *"power"* or *"desire"* which can be dated back to a time in ancient Greek history when the truth of a discourse coincided with the power of whoever uttered it. At this time claims to validity and claims to power were inseparably interwoven in a state which, in Foucault's view, takes on the appearance of an implicitly privileged world free of ideology, as it were.

> True discourse—in the meaningful sense—inspiring respect and terror, to which all were obliged to submit, because it held sway over all and was pronounced by men who spoke as of right, according to ritual, meting out justice and attributed to each his

rightful share; it prophesied the future, not merely announcing what was going to occur, but contributing to its actual event, carrying men along with it and thus weaving itself into the fabric of fate.[3]

The validity of such discourses is purely empirical; it relies on the potential for sanctions that the power elite have at their disposal. Without a moment's hesitation Foucault accepts a conception of truth that cannot be integrated within any theory of truth. Strictly speaking, discussion of truth at all would be inappropriate in this context. Foucault is naturally aware of this. But the point his theory aims at is precisely a Nietzschean one—to unmask the conceptual framework of our intellectual tradition by contrasting the will to knowledge and power/desire:

> And yet, a century later, the highest truth no longer resided in what discourse *was*, nor in what it *did*: it lay in what was *said*. The day dawned when truth moved over from the ritualised act—potent and just—of enunciation to settle on what was enunciated itself: its meaning, its form, its object and its relation to what it referred to. A division emerged between Hesiod and Plato, separating true discourse from false; it was a new division for, henceforth, true discourse was no longer considered precious and desirable, since it had ceased to be discourse linked to the exercise of power. And so the Sophists were routed.[4]

The process of separating true and false retains a key role in Foucault's theory, informing the approach of his studies on power and determining how the two concepts of power are to be contrasted. The systematic critique of the human sciences that was presented in *The Order of Things* is completed here genealogically. One could say that the will to knowledge conducts itself with regard to the human sciences roughly as power conducts itself with regard to *episteme*. Once again it is a matter of unmasking the kind of thinking that conceives truth as the truth of the Order of Things. Foucault relocates to the beginnings of philosophical thought that which Bachelard saw as a mistake of realism and of traditional, substantialist epistemology. Foucault sees Plato as the author of the distinction between essence and appearance and between true and false; he finds, in this "doubling" of the world, the thematic area wherein genealogy can exert its subversive force. In "Theatrum philosophicum,"[5] an article devoted to Deleuze and influenced by his line of questioning, Plato's bequest is thought to be that he established identitarian thought.[6] According to Foucault's reading, the allegedly chaotic stream of events forces Plato to a hierarchy that is both theoretical and moral: he establishes both a world order and moral thinking.

> The tyranny of good will, the obligation to think "in common" with others . . . the exclusion of stupidity—the disreputable morality of thought whose function in our society is easy to decipher. We must liberate ourselves from these constraints; and in perverting this morality, philosophy itself is disoriented.[7]

For Foucault-the-Nietzschean, subverting this characterization of Platonic thinking requires making it clear that philosophy as a whole, not just the human sciences, has fallen into an anthropological sleep. It requires returning to an ideal point in time prior to the Platonic doubling of the world and finding an unbiased and productive way of thinking there.

> Rather, we should welcome the cunning assembly that simulates and clamors at the door. And what will enter, submerging appearance and breaking its engagement to essence, will be the event; the incorporeal will dissipate the density of matter; a timeless insistence will destroy the circle that imitates eternity; an impenetrable singularity will divest itself of the contamination by purity; the actual semblance of

the simulacrum will support the falseness of false appearances. The Sophist springs up, and challenges Socrates to prove that he is not the illegitimate usurper.[8]

The dualistic conceptualization of power in "The Discourse on Language" serves to synthesize the ambivalence found in the early Foucault's conceptualization of the history of culture. At the end of the semiological period, what was still seen in the 1954 foreword and in *Madness and Civilization* as an immediate and incompatible juxtaposition of the dream or of madness on the one hand with their structural analysis[9] on the other returns in the form of a dualism within power itself. Now, however, the systematic relation between the two attitudes can be demonstrated. The Apollo and Dionysus of Foucault-the-genealogist are constructed out of the tension between an ontological, normative power and its historically determined form found in the will to knowledge. I define the will to power as a substantialist conception of power because its main characteristic consists in referring to a substantialist conception of truth. Foucault articulates the conflict between the two forms of power vis-à-vis the concept of truth as follows:

> If, since the time of the Greeks, true discourse no longer responds to desire or to that which exercises power in the will to truth, in the will to speak out in true discourse, what, then, is at work, if not desire and power? True discourse liberated by the nature of its form from desire and power is incapable of recognizing the will to truth which pervades it; and the will to truth, having imposed itself upon us for so long, is such that the truth it seeks to reveal cannot fail to mask it.[10]

Now as always, power and desire are at work behind the historically determined form of power as will to knowledge; they serve as the no longer recognizable and yet indispensable sources of every event. Thus it is the task of the genealogist to liberate power and desire from this burden by analyzing the descent of the will to knowledge.

Only the will to knowledge can be analyzed genealogically and can be the object of an investigation that raises quasi-scientific claims. For, while the sphere of power/desire can be experienced, at best, it cannot be made the object of a conceptual analysis. Thus, the will to knowledge belongs to a different level of analysis. It is not a concept based in a theory of instinctual drives; it is not rooted in the nervous system of life. Rather, it is the historical and, as such, analyzable form of our cultural development.

The first major empirical study of this period, *Discipline and Punish*, only addresses power as will to knowledge. This has resulted in many interpreters being misled into advancing the thesis that Foucault advocates a monistic conception of power.

Descent and Emergence:
The Dualism within Genealogy

After the relatively explicit theses in "The Discourse on Language," Foucault no longer discusses a counter-force, some kind of a Dionysian moment that could balance out the normalizing and disciplinary force of power in the form of the will to knowledge. Foucault is unmistakable in this regard; he criticizes

> the view that one must rediscover the things themselves in their original liveliness behind power, behind its acts of force and its perfidities: that one must rediscover the spontaneity of madness behind the isolating walls, the productive disturbances of delinquency through the bars of the penal system, the purity of desire in the sexual prohibitions.[11]

When one limits oneself to *Discipline and Punish*,[12] the thesis of a power monism seems to be supported insofar as power takes on the role of the sole heuristic category for analyzing the structural conditions necessary for the emergence of societies. Indeed, in many places it seems to be even the sole category for understanding history at all. Yet even *Discipline and Punish*, with its prima facie strongly monistic character, can be read differently when this important book is viewed not as the consummate result of Foucault's deliberations on power, but rather as part of a "work in progress" that encompassed much of the 1970s. This supposition holds true above all when one seeks, via an analysis of method, that is, of the genealogical writing of history, to obtain insight concerning possible differences in access, indirectly but also in the object itself, that is, in the concept of power. The 1971 essay, "Nietzsche, Genealogy, History,"[13] presents itself as the most important methodological study of power for pursuing this concern. There, the concepts power, body, and truth appear in a systematic manner for the first time, although they are not described in detail. They form a theoretical network that can serve as a backdrop for the later writings.[14]

The Nietzsche essay is one of the few works in which Foucault does not address an author from the perspective of a historian, but rather addresses the author's arguments. Its primary goal is to render the features of the genealogical writing of history more precise; it thereby emphasizes both the similarities to and the differences from Nietzsche's approach. Foucault's basic thesis is that Nietzsche, in his genealogical writings, failed to clearly distinguish between descent (*Herkunft*) and emergence (*Entstehung*). In Foucault's version of genealogy these two concepts, which were introduced by Nietzsche, albeit unsystematically, are raised to the status of the main pillars of genealogy.

Foucault delineates multiple aspects of that which the genealogist designates by "descent." Descent fragments ego-identity in that the unity of ego-identity points to the heterogeneity of its moments; it discloses the causality of that which is the ground of our certitude; it demonstrates—in a direct continuation of the epistemological themes found throughout Foucault's writings—that that which seems to be given does not harbor a hidden truth that could provide the knower with a secure foundation.

The search for descent is not the erecting of foundations: on the contrary, it disturbs what was previously considered immobile; it fragments what was thought unified; it shows the heterogeneity of what was imagined consistent with itself.[15]

But the most important feature of Foucault's interpretation of descent is its relation to the body problematic. If the term "origin" (*Ursprung*) designates belief in the existence of a pure essence or truth, the continuity of an idea, the unity of identity despite the contingency of historical events, then the genealogical critique of the body, on the other hand, acts as the unmasking reverse side of the idealistic and substantialistic fiction represented by a philosophy of origins.

The body—and every thing that touches it: diet, climate, and soil—is the domain of the *Herkunft*. The body manifests the stigmata of past experience and also gives rise to desires, failings, and errors. . . . The body is the inscribed surface of events (traced by language and dissolved by ideas), the locus of a dissociated self (adopting the illusion of a substantial unity), and a volume in perpetual disintegration.[16]

The analysis of descent carries out a function within genealogy which could be called a critique of ideology in the broadest sense of the term: The inscription of previous life experiences on the body permits something like an unrelenting history of the individual to be read from the body, as well as allowing the consolation offered by a philosophy of origins to be unmasked as illusory.

The concept "emergence" designates the second object domain of genealogy; it takes into account the dynamic moment in which new historical constellations are formed. Emergence is the "principle and the singular law of an apparition."[17] If the analysis of descent breaks with the idea of continuity in history, then emergence places the finality of history in question.

> In placing present needs at the origin, the metaphysician would convince us of an obscure purpose that seeks its realization at the moment it arises. Genealogy, however, seeks to reestablish the various systems of subjection: not the anticipatory power of meaning, but the hazardous play of dominations.[18]

The search for emergence claims to describe efforts at pure mastery that follow the model of warlike confrontations. Analyzed through the lens of emergence, war becomes the basic feature common to each historical event; not only public conflicts, but also every normative structure that tries to secure a common human life is derived from the model of the warlike confrontation. Social forms of common life, institutions, and rules in general are reduced to provisional moments of taking stock within an ongoing conflict situation.[19] Many aspects of such an understanding of the concept of rule and of history as a permanent state of war could be criticized; I will return to this point later. What is of immediate relevance for the development of Foucault's theory, however, seems to me to be the epistemological significance of his conception of emergence. That is, the point here is not to describe the emergence *of* something, but rather to describe the process of emergence itself.

> What Nietzsche calls the *Entstehungsherd* of the concept of goodness is not specifically the energy of the strong or the reaction of the weak, but precisely this scene where they are superimposed or face-to-face.[20]

The concept of emergence is of particular importance for interpreting Foucault's genealogy because its definition reveals a divergence from Nietzsche's genealogy that has systematic relevance. Dreyfus and Rabinow conceived the difference between the two genealogical approaches as follows:

> Foucault the genealogist is no longer outraged, as was Nietzsche, by the discovery that the claim of objectivity masks subjective motivations. Foucault is interested in how both scientific objectivity and subjective intentions emerge together in a space set up not by individuals but by social practices.[21]

The fact that emergence is conceived by Foucault in the special sense of *Entstehungsherd* indicates that the practical projects of acting subjects—which are far removed from the psychological focus of perspectivism—are subordinate to the abstract technology of social power practices.

Of course, in examining Foucault's interpretation of Nietzsche, we should not overlook the fact that Foucault's genealogy, precisely by its thematization of the individual as actor, importantly enriches his earlier approach. Namely, in Foucault's earlier scientific writings individuals were conceptualized solely as mere functions of a constellation of signs that determined historical development; now they shift to the foreground, thematically as well as methodologically.

Thematically, the historical process whereby embodied subjects are individuated, which is the historical condition necessary both for the emergence of the human sciences and for the development of capitalist means of production,[22] becomes the central object of Foucault's studies. Methodologically, the idea of power practices unavoidably alludes to the at least implicit action-theoretical background of his theory. It also leaves open the possibility that Foucault, on the basis of his initial concept of the subject, will come to understand that his theory belongs to the object domain he is investigating and thus will escape at least the more blatant forms of a performative contradiction. At a later point these considerations will force Foucault, out of inner necessity as it were, to further self-corrections with regard to the subjectivity problematic.[23] Nevertheless, the difference between Nietzsche's and Foucault's conception of the subject, which was recognized by Dreyfus and Rabinow, signals a problem that is of consequence for the entire interpretation of power in Foucault. A quotation will explain the problem better:

> As descent qualifies the strength or weakness of an instinct and its inscription on a body, emergence designates a place of confrontation but not as a closed field offering the spectacle of a struggle among equals. Rather . . . it is a "non-place," a pure distance, which indicates that the adversaries do not belong to a common space.[24]

Subjective motivations barely play a role in this account of emergence. Indeed, this model of the confrontation between social actors can no longer admit that actors are reduced to functions of the system in which they act because the entire system ultimately consists of their numerous micro-struggles. In spite of this, war is not entirely appropriate as an explanatory framework in this context either because the confrontation does not take place in a common pregiven "battleground," which would have allowed the distinction to be made between structural conditions and particular actors. For the opponents, as well, there is no common ground, for in this peculiar power struggle the ground itself (that is, the structural conditions) is in question. It changes in the course of the confrontation, as do the opponents. Because they do not fight in an arena that is defined once and for all, they do not have any hard and fast affiliations; they are not even tied to a hard and fast identity—both are context-dependent. The fact that such a conception of emergence cannot be attributed to anyone is merely the result of this model.

By understanding emergence as *Entstehungsherd*, Foucault interprets Nietzsche's insight in a manner that takes up the structure of discourse found in *The Archaeology of Knowledge* as well as picking up on the earlier conceptions of the dream and of madness.[25] Here, as in the earlier works, a historical field is defined whose elements, the context that they form and the rules that they structure, are categorically described as homogenous and inseparable from one another. Thus, the concept of emergence seems to repeat, in a new form, Foucault's original figure of thought, that of an anonymous and categorically indefinable complex acting as the historical a priori. If this interpretation of emergence is correct, then it points to a concept of power which, unlike the power that is the object of the analysis of descent, does not represent an established, ideological camouflaging of history in need of unmasking. Rather, it should render the actual dynamics of social processes visible—and that by way of impulses that cannot be traced back to subjective interests or to the subjective motivational complex of individuals. This allows some problems to become more precise and others to take on a new form.

For one, the distinction between the analysis of descent and the analysis of emergence in the genealogical writing of history now lets us draw some general conclusions regarding the concept of power. The Nietzsche essay and the subsequent writings actually do not contain a fundamental dualism in the sense of two opposed forms of power or two opposed principles, whose conflict could be said to fuel the historical dynamic. For Foucault there is only one power. Things look different, however, when power is viewed in its historically determined form. In this case, the methodological distinction between descent and emergence points to a corresponding distinction in the concept of power itself which, in turn, provides an important criterion for understanding Foucault's theory.

Namely, the analysis of descent presupposes a form of power that is characterized by its constituting or individuating function. Only the historical configurations of the will to knowledge—the soul, identity, the continuity of the human substance throughout the course of historical events—could be unmasked by the analysis of descent. For its part, this genealogical unmasking is only possible if one accepts the premise that *the will to knowledge portrays a historically contingent and thus reversible constellation of power*, even though this constellation has prevailed for more than two thousand years and has solidified only gradually.

The analysis of emergence, on the other hand, presupposes a form of power that is operative in the strategic confrontation of individual actors. That is, in Foucault's material analyses this diffuse power is tightly interwoven with the epistemological paradigm of the will to knowledge. It is interwoven such that the will to knowledge must presuppose the model of warlike confrontation, while marking its form and direction in turn. As a result, this aspect of emergence, as well, seems to be a moment typical of the strategic confrontation and thus can be thoroughly integrated into the dynamic of the will to knowledge. By analytically distinguishing between these two aspects of the analysis of power, the possibility is at least implicitly left open that in a *different* historical constellation individual actors' strategic level of power would not necessarily have to be exercised in the form of a will to knowledge. The power that comes to light as a result of the genealogist's analysis of emergence implicitly raises an explanatory claim that runs counter to the will to knowledge: That is, that the thesis of the continuous civil war should be valid for all epochs.

For another, this suggestion regarding the dualism of power requires a more thoroughgoing analysis of Foucault's studies on the theory of power, one that will substantiate the hypothesis regarding the two forms of power and that will make possible an investigation of their systematic relation. The questions that are raised by this preliminary inquiry into the problematic of the two forms of power are: "What features distinguish and can plausibly differentiate the model of power as will to knowledge from power as a warlike confrontation?" and "Can such an analytic articulation of the concept of power contribute to a systematic understanding of Foucault's theory?" In addressing these questions I will be guided by the three Bachelardian motifs as they were utilized in earlier chapters. I will try to explain power as the will to knowledge via the epistemological critique of the traditional epistemological line of questioning, while the strategic aspect of power will be reconciled to the motifs of the epistemological break as well as to the pre-individualistic creative subjectivity.

The Will to Knowledge and Traditional Epistemology

Discipline and Punish is an imposing critique of two theses that are deeply rooted in the Marxist and in the humanistic readings of history in particular; that is, it is critical of the thesis that enlightenment and humanization in life relations are indicative of the progressive development of freer forms of life, and it is critical of the understanding of power as repressive. In the specific context of a history of the prison, this critique claims that the reformers' approach, which made the treatment of delinquents more humane by abolishing brutal methods, should not be understood as implementing higher moral values. Rather, it can be traced back to the formation and refinement not of a repressive, but of a productive, form of power. The critique of the, in Foucault's opinion, supposedly progressive implications of the Enlightenment and the critique of the conception of power as oppression, which seem to be far removed from one another, prove to be related when they are seen from the perspective of an epistemological attitude that is critical of knowledge, that is, is anti-substantialist.

Clearly, Foucault is not vexed with the agents of the Enlightenment due to their sympathetic pity for the misery of creatures suffering from physical distress, such as criminals or vagabonds who have fallen under the disciplinary yoke of state power. After all, Foucault's collected work, the spontaneous perlocutionary effect of his writings, so to speak, is driven by a similar pathos. Rather, his critique is grounded in his conviction that the outrage manifested by the agents of the Enlightenment ultimately has other grounds; that is, it is carried out in the name of an abstract conception of humanity. "In the worst of murderers, there is one thing, at least, to be respected when one punishes: his 'humanity.'"[26] This critique is directed at the ideal, attributed to the humanists, that something like a "human substance" can be found in each individual that should be respected despite any appearance of criminality. Thus, one can say that according to the Foucauldian interpretation, the agents of Enlightenment are trapped in a variant of the realistic fallacy which, together with a substantialist idea of humanity, provides the premises necessary for the emergence both of the will to knowledge and of the human sciences.

His critique of power, understood as repression, is carried out in a similar and complementary manner. First of all, Foucault rejects the idea that power is something that one can possess. Namely, he presupposes that power

> [exercised on the body is conceived] not as a property, but as a strategy. . . . In short this power is exercised rather than possessed; it is not the "privilege," acquired or preserved, of the dominant class, but the overall effect of its strategic positions. . . .[27]

The rejection of the metaphor of possession establishes the premises necessary for the critique of power as repression. Namely, if one denies that power can be attributed to someone in the manner of a possession, then its effect cannot be understood as a prohibition of that which would be permitted to the power elite. "We must cease once and for all to describe the effects of power in negative terms: it 'excludes,' it 'represses,' it 'censors,' it 'abstracts,' it 'masks,' it 'conceals.'"[28] In Foucault's discussion this thesis constitutes a kind of reverse side to the critique of Enlightenment humanism. Both the humanistic pathos regarding the dignity of humanity as well as the metaphor of power as possession and repression result from conceiving of individual substance as something that must be protected if it is not to become an object of oppression. In both cases it is thought that the human essence of the recipients of these views can be defined once and for all. This should provide the criteria that determine whether they are respected or oppressed. In Foucault's eyes, talk of human dignity and of its injury or abasement should be criticized because it assumes an ideological object, that is, a "subject," that is naively thought to be readily definable.

Foucault does not see that the contents of the Enlightenment could have been obtained from figures of thought *other* than that of a self-referential philosophy of consciousness.[29] His rejection of reform and of the concept of power as repressive is a logical result of the fact that Foucault, like Nietzsche, assimilates Enlightenment thought to the metaphysical tradition and then examines and criticizes this tradition only from the perspective of a critique of knowledge. The extent of Bachelard's influence, which served as the basis first for criticizing the human sciences and now for criticizing the newly introduced power/knowledge complex, can be measured on this preliminary systematization of the prison problematic. As for the rest, the descent of Foucault's approach from the critique of knowledge can be read in the otherwise strange claim his theory of power raises, to write a "common history of power relations and object relations."[30] From this interpretive standpoint the systematic necessity of this "common history" becomes clear.

The range of Foucault's critique, however, is not limited to an epistemologically oriented critique of substantialism or metaphysics, adapted to the model of disciplinary power. Rather, this critique is presupposed, for the aim of *Discipline and Punish* first becomes apparent when humanism and the thesis of repressive power, with their associated ideological status, are reconciled with the actual dynamic of power understood as the will to knowledge. For, in Foucault's eyes, the vehemence with which the agents of the Enlightenment insist on the inviolability of humanity lacks the innocence of a false thesis that has an insecure epistemological basis. Rather, this thesis, along with the human sciences that are derived from it, such as psychiatry, criminology, and criminal law, is one of the components that constitutes the will to knowledge as the "political technology of the body." With the aid of the concept of power that has now been introduced, Foucault scrutinizes the form of the human sciences that was analyzed and criticized in *The Order of Things* and articulates two of its aspects— with reference to disciplinary control and with reference to the increase of knowledge:

> This "man," discovered in the criminal, would become the target of penal intervention, the object that it claimed to correct and transform, the domain of a whole series of "criminological" sciences and strange "penitentiary" practices.[31]

In the common history of power relations and knowledge relations, the realistic fallacy and the refinement of methods of control complement each other. They form a decentralized, functional complex that steadily augments a power that enters into every aspect of society, thereby introducing processes of subjection that lead to increased individuation. By striving for complete control over bodily behavior, power constitutes ever new aspects of and deeper levels of the individual's inwardness which it, however, falsely views as largely predetermined. According to Foucault, the regulation of time, the analysis of bodily motions, the entering of biographical events into bureaucratic archives, and the classification and gradation of sanctions are the elements whose interplay forms the network out of which the subject, in the modern sense of the word, is produced. In Foucault's exemplary analysis, the prison, along with the school, the hospital, the barracks, and the factory, becomes one of the complexes of norms, institutions, and architectonic solutions that prepared and made possible the political implementation of the modern social order in the form of the technology of power prevalent today.

Foucault chooses the term "panopticism" to designate this political technology of the body:

> at the periphery, an annular building; at the centre, a tower; this tower is pierced with wide windows that open onto the inner side of the ring; the peripheric building is divided into cells, each of which extends the whole width of the building; they have two windows, one on the inside, corresponding to the windows of the tower; the other, on the outside, allows the light to cross the cell from one end to the other. All that is needed, then, is to place a supervisor in a central tower and to shut up in each cell a madman, a patient, a condemned man, a worker or a schoolboy. By the effect of backlighting, one can observe from the tower, standing out precisely against the light, the small captive shadows in the cells of the periphery.[32]

With this well-known reference to Bentham's panopticon, Foucault has found an example that includes all the major features of power as will to knowledge: Due to the structure of the installation, surveillance is permanent and proceeds almost automatically. In this way power is de-individualized: It is constantly in operation, independent of the attributes of the supervisor, and its effect is an abstract one. The less it depends on applying immediate force the more effective it is.

But even more interesting than its disciplinary function is the panopticon's production of knowledge. It can serve "as a machine to carry out experiments, to alter behaviour, to train or correct individuals."[33] The panopticon is best suited to "experiment with medicines," "carry out different punishments," and "teach different techniques"; in short, one can experiment with the most diverse techniques of manipulation. In one passage Foucault defines Bentham's panopticon as "a kind of laboratory of power."[34] This forceful characterization, which elucidates the disciplinary and the knowledge-productive aspects of his conception of

power in one breath, can be developed, in our line of interpretation, such that it provides further confirmation for the
thesis that Foucault's theory of power is descended from a
critique of knowledge.[35] Namely, following his line of argumentation to the point where the panoptical function
becomes the generalized model of power in modern societies suggests that in such a society of generalized panopticism power itself becomes a laboratory, namely, a laboratory
for the processes of individuation. In Foucault's hands
inwardness, the sphere of the "soul" that Foucault examines
historically[36]—from the first practices of confession to those
of psychoanalysis—is transformed into the product of power
interventions.

> This is the historical reality of this soul, which,
> unlike the soul represented by Christian theology,
> is not born in sin and subject to punishment, but is
> born rather out of methods of punishment, supervi-
> sion and constraint. This real, non-corporal soul is
> not a substance; it is the element in which are artic-
> ulated the effects of a certain type of power and the
> reference of a certain type of knowledge, the machin-
> ery by which the power relations give rise to a pos-
> sible corpus of knowledge, and knowledge extends
> and reinforces the effects of this power.[37]

Foucault makes the bold claim that power strategies stand
in a direct causal relation to the reflective knowledge of
everyday experience, which is understood as a mere effect.
The considerable burden of proof required by this implausible supposition is not provided.[38] This fact, however, is not
the only weakness in his conceptualization of processes of
individuation. The definition of the concept of the body is
another weakness, one which is related to the topic of the
individual.

On the one hand, Foucault must stress the relative
importance of disciplinary interventions on the body in
order to sustain his critique of every variant on the ideal of
discovering a continuity or a unity of the self that stays the

same throughout all historical changes, be that in the form of identity, cultural tradition, or some other form of asserting that there is a substantial human essence. On the other hand, a similar problem is raised when it is a matter of liberating the body from every remainder of a substantialist or anthropological understanding. Foucault explicitly rejects this understanding. In an essay on Nietzsche he writes:

> Effective history differs from traditional history in being without constants. Nothing in man—not even his body—is sufficiently stable to serve as the basis for self-recognition or for understanding other men.[39]

The genealogical writing of history cannot take recourse in a foundational moment, not even one that takes on naturalistic or vitalistic tendencies; it "deprives the self of the reassuring stability of life and nature."[40] Guided by these principles, an indeterminate theoretical status is attributed to the body. Despite its initial strategic role in Foucault's system, in the final analysis it seems to be little more than a gray zone, a material substrate that, due to the fact that it cannot be defined, is only fit to be molded by the will to knowledge. This calls to mind the similarly unclear status that Bachelard ascribed to nature in his historical epistemology. According to Bachelard's theory, nature has no truths of its own, no wealth of substantial attributes awaiting discovery; rather, it is constituted and technologically produced by scientific spirit.

In this problem area as well one can see how Foucault transposed Bachelard's epistemology of the natural sciences onto the topic of the individual without attending to the actual character of the theory of power's object domain. Foucault views the body only as an epistemological object, one that can be thematized genealogically, by way of reconstructing the objectifications of power. The price of such a characterization is a completely counterintuitive truncation of the concept of the individual to the point where it is a mere screen onto which disciplinary and objectifying practices are projected. As implausible as it may seem, Foucault must simply ignore all elements that allude to identity, to the normative content of lifeworld relations as found in everyday life experience. In the attempt to overcome the aporetic compulsion towards foundationalism found in the philosophy of consciousness and especially in phenomenology,[41] Foucault's theory fails to cross the innovative threshold marked by Husserl's introduction of the concept "lifeworld" into philosophical discussion.[42] Because Foucault adheres to Bachelard's schema of the critique of knowledge and transposes it from historical epistemology first to the domain of the human sciences and then to the domain of a theory of society, he is able to describe processes of individuation, such as labor uprisings, only as processes of manipulation or objectification.

Power and Life-Practice

The difficulties Foucault encountered when he tried to replace the lifeworld background of daily practice with an epistemological conceptual schema reappear when he tries to provide information about the pragmatic dimension of social power practices. There, in the context attributed to the genealogical analysis of emergence, the will to knowledge relinquishes its place in favor of a schema in which power practices represent a network of countless strategies "from below" that are subject to a micrological analysis. Even here, every possible connection between power and the complexes of meaning proffered by the lifeworld is excluded, even though the bearers of power strategies are clearly identified with the actors of social practice. The Bachelardian motif of the epistemological break, if understood as an extended critique of the foundationalism found in the lifeworld, remains a basic motif for Foucault's entire system, even during the period concerned with power. Hence the description of power practices as events, that is, as anonymous occurrences that cannot be traced back to one final motivation and that, in their haphazard development, prove to be the driving force of history as well as the active moment in the formation of social objects.

To be sure, the Foucault of the micrology of power has different interests and investigates different objects than the author of *The Order of Things* or *The Archaeology of Knowledge*. He is no longer mainly concerned with a critical analysis of the human sciences and their relative importance vis-à-vis science and everyday experience. His target is no longer the knowledge that was criticized in the early semiological writings. As a result, it is difficult to understand this insistence on the epistemological break, a topic closely related to the problematic of scientific theory. Nonetheless, this aspect of Foucault's theoretical schema as well remains essentially unchanged by the transition to a theory of society and the theory of power.

As already mentioned, Foucault orients himself on the model of the warlike confrontation, a model that should be able to take into account the specific form of each of the micro-events found in the social network. As a result, the commonplaces of everyday life and the rules that organize the normative structure of life practice will not simply be ignored, but will be used polemically. That is, they will be deliberately used as a target for his strategic conception of power practices. "Rules are empty in themselves, violent and unfinalized; they are impersonal and can be bent to any purpose."[43] In an interview in which he was asked about the relation of genealogy to the French phenomenological tradition and to Marxism, Foucault replied decisively:

> I don't believe the problem can be solved by historicising the subject as posited by the phenomenologists, fabricating a subject that evolves through the course of history. One has to dispense with the constituent subject, to get rid of the subject itself, that's to say, to arrive at an analysis which can account for the constitution of the subject within a historical framework.[44]

That does not mean, however, that Foucault thereby advocates a form of vitalism, as may have been the case in

Madness and Civilization or even in "The Discourse on Language." As has been already shown, the example of the body makes this especially clear.

> We believe, in any event, that the body obeys the exclusive laws of physiology and that it escapes the influence of history, but this too is false. The body is molded by a great many distinct regimes.[45]

The discussion of regimes[46] in effect guarantees that any pairing of power practices with biological, physiological, or any other necessities required for the survival of the species remain out of the question.

Foucault's epistemological attitude forbids him any kind of fixed orientation in historical events. Due to this postulate, the formulation of Foucault's genealogy has to be even more radical than Nietzsche's. Each suggestion of instrumentalism, each Darwinistic influence, must be banned from this theory, the major feature of which, now as ever, is its critique of the givenness of things, even when this "givenness" only has a weak intrinsic character, as is the case with the necessities that serve to sustain life.[47] Thus, power practices cannot be understood instrumentally, according to Foucault. They do not contain any elements that could be distinguished by their "usefulness for life,"[48] as Nietzsche called it, because this would seem to retain an indirect theoretical foundation, which is unacceptable to Foucault. In the period of his reflection concerned with power practices, as in the earlier writings on *epistemes* or discourse, Foucault advocates the idea of an abstract praxis that represents the occurrence of anonymous signpost events. It is the anchoring of this practice in lifeworld relations that should be unmasked as deceptive.

> We want historians to confirm our belief that the present rests upon profound intentions and immutable necessities. . . . But the true historical sense confirms our existence among countless lost events, without a landmark or a point of reference.[49]

The Creative A Priori

By characterizing power as an event, Foucault again faces a problem that was raised in his semiological period, one that reformulating his theory in terms of power should have resolved: The problem of the pragmatic status of statements. It was shown in the discussion of *The Archaeology of Knowledge* that the statement was overburdened with a performative dimension which, although necessary to maintain the autonomy of discourse, led to insurmountable aporias that were ultimately beyond the scope of the analysis of signs as a whole.[50] Thus, setting up power as the new systematic focal point for Foucault's theory was interpreted as an attempt to locate that practice which, in the structuralist writings, was relegated to the domains of *episteme* or to discourse through a kind of abstractive fallacy, in a field of power practices that can be analyzed micrologically and that are carried out by individual actors. It was also shown, however, that Foucault's understanding of power merely shunted aside rather than resolved the unsolved question regarding the pragmatic status of the historical a priori, be it *episteme* or discourse. The two concepts of power, between which at least an analytic distinction can be made in the writings on power, do not offer a satisfactory basis for explaining the social dynamic. That is, the will to knowledge, which was analyzed primarily in terms of a genealogy of descent, and power practices, which were addressed from the perspective of a genealogy of emergence, do not offer a satisfactory basis for explaining the pragmatic dimension of a historical a priori that has now been expanded to include a theory of society.

The will to knowledge cannot provide such an explanation because it only represents a historically determined form of the constitution of social and cultural artifacts. The will to knowledge or to truth, with its structural similarity to the conceptual schema of the human sciences, is nothing more than an extension of the social scientific "turn" that introduced the "anthropological sleep." The fact that this turn is expanded from the narrow domain of the human sciences to the broader field of social analysis, coupled with the fact that its birth at the beginning of modernity is dated back, in good Nietzschean style, to the beginnings of Greek metaphysics, does not change the fact that this is a matter of a figure of thought that is historically limited and epistemologically determined. Thus, it provides information about the historical form whereby social artifacts were practically constituted, but not about the practice in which such processes of objectification take place.

Within Foucault's model, it is more likely that power practices will be able to provide this explanation, and this is more likely at the point when they, in the context of a genealogy of emergence, are investigated with regard to the dynamic dimension of the constant war that takes place within all articulations of the historical or social process. In contrast to the semiological understanding of history which avoids their "violent, bloody and lethal character,"[51] individual actors appear here as physical bearers of power.

> Power acts through the smallest elements: the family, sexual relations, but also: residential relations, neighbourhoods, etc. As far as we go in the social network, we always find power as something which "runs through" it, that acts, that brings about effects. It becomes effective or not, that is, power is always a definite form of momentary and constantly reproduced encounters among a definite number of individuals.[52]

The network of micro-struggles, which is what power ultimately consists of, includes confrontations within the family, at work, and between the sexes.

Next to such a construction of the theory of power one would expect to find a corresponding theory of action that would provide the conceptual apparatus necessary for analyzing the structural characteristics of social practice. Foucault, however, does not take up such questions. Certainly, he must implicitly make a number of presuppositions regarding the action (*Handeln*) of social actors; these emerge between the lines of his studies.⁵³ However, he must ignore these assumptions, regardless of what form they take because, due to their substantialist implications, they would contradict his approach to power and to processes of individuation.

Because his approach cannot admit that action has significance for his theory, the historical a priori is left with carrying this burden.

To summarize: The analysis of signs found in the earlier writings failed plausibly to explain the pragmatic value of the historical a priori, which was conceived in terms of *episteme* or discourse. By making the concept of power, or power practices, the new focus of Foucault's theory, a venue seemed to be created whereby the ever present intuition of a holistic, pragmatic historical a priori could be spelled out. Nonetheless, even this new framework seems to be inadequate to the task. In the form of the will to knowledge, power represents a merely epistemological figure of thought which presupposes the dynamics of practices rather than explains them. Power practices, understood on the model of a diffuse war, as a constant struggle carried out by individuals, contributes little to understanding social processes because it is claimed that, on the one hand, the actors are the result of the processes of individuation carried out by the will to knowledge, but on the other hand, they are said to be without structural motivations for action.

Foucault is well aware that his depiction of power practices as the motor driving historical processes leaves some questions unanswered. Let us now return to the *Archaeology*'s unresolved question regarding the pragmatic status of statements, a question which should have been resolved by the theory of power. The difficulties remain. The main thesis of the *Archaeology* was that the statement was constituted by rules of formation which, in turn, consisted of statements. This central intuition, which resulted in a leveling of context and ground, as well as leading to Foucault's greatest theory-immanent difficulty, reappears in the relation between individuals and power practices. As statements, in the archaeological context, are said to be constituted by rules of formation, while these rules are said to consist only of statements, so are individuals literally constituted by power practices. For their part, however, these practices are only to be understood via the action of individuals.

> In fact, it [the individual] is already one of the prime effects of power that certain bodies, certain gestures, certain discourses, certain desires, come to be identified and constituted as individuals. The individual, that is, is not the *vis-à-vis* of power; it is, I believe, one of its prime effects. The individual is an effect of power, and at the same time, or precisely to the extent to which it is that effect, it is the element of its articulation. The individual which power has constituted is at the same time its vehicle.[54]

Foucault gives the name "apparatus" [*dispositif*] to this unusual coupling of empirical action, which has been reduced to the strategic level of individuals, with constitutive power practices. This choice of terms no doubt works. Namely, an apparatus of security or of control more or less denotes the pragmatic dimension of an institution. That is, it denotes the totality of organizational or hierarchical structures, technical equipment, and human action that is necessary to manage or prevent a crisis. For example, an apparatus is everything that must be used in combination in order to make possible the mobilization of the fire company, from the initial call to extinguishing the fire—the telephone, fire company, special trucks, traffic laws, training, and individual skill. The aspect of apparatus that interests Foucault, even beyond its use in everyday language, is its categorical heterogeneity. This heterogeneity does not prevent Foucault from understanding apparatus as a closed complex for which intentional action is necessary, but not sufficient, to ensure its anonymous, quasi-automatic functioning.

As impressive as such a conception of apparatus may be as a symbolic figure for social analysis, this model does not offer any new elements that could shore up the traditional weaknesses of Foucault's theory. Disposition is merely a translation of the concept "discourse" into the language of a theory of society. Now as ever, Foucault's model is trapped in the untenable position of having to renounce a clear distinction between empirical and transcendental moments without wanting to relinquish the supple capacities of an analysis constructed as a theory of constitution. For that reason Foucault must insist that power practices (like rules of formation) constitute individuals (like statements) but that, viewed analytically, they do not manifest a status that is in principle rule-bound and nonempirical and that would allow them to be categorically differentiated once and for all. Thus, despite the expansion of his theory to include both individual actors and power practices, the abstract character that was established already in *The Archaeology of Knowledge* with the catchphrase "autonomy of discourse" cannot be overcome. Two aspects of the claim raised by the theory of power are not redeemed, that is, to include practice within its system and to make it the centerpoint of the theory. For one, the practice of social actors is reduced to strategic action, which renders an understanding of identity formation and of cognitive and practical processes of learning, as well as the cohesion of this version of social relations, nearly impossible.[55] For another, the observation that individual character is constituted by power practices amounts to saying that even this impoverished, instrumental model of individual practice depends on the transformations brought about by the still abstract intervention of power in the form of the will to knowledge. Ultimately, then, the latitude apparently granted to individual action in the face of the fateful rise of the practices of the will to knowledge is withdrawn.

Power must be analyzed as something which circulates, or rather as something which only functions in the form of a chain. It is never localized here or there, never in anybody's hands. . . . Power is employed and exercised through a net-like organization. And not only do individuals circulate between its threads; they are always in the position of simultaneously undergoing and exercising this power. They are not only its inert or consenting target; they are always also the elements of its articulation.[56]

Reduced to mere elements articulated by a superior power, the individual can contribute very little to the unfolding of practice because, according to Foucault's theory, the only place for practice is within the relational machinery of supraindividual power practices.

I would now like to make some concluding remarks and address some of the questions raised earlier regarding the applicability of the Bachelardian theme of creative subjectivity to the theory of power.

The will to knowledge together with power practices can be interpreted as a binary system that provides the conditions of possibility for historical formations. The former establishes a historically determined framework that includes both discursive and institutional moments. The latter represents its dynamic background, which draws on relations of force. This doubled, quasi-transcendental model should make it possible to accommodate both the "structuralist" and the performative dimensions of Foucault's theory, both of which took the form of an unmediated intuition in Foucault's early writings.[57] It seems that the difficulties of the earlier attempts could be resolved by a division of labor determined by function. The will to knowledge has relations that can be analyzed empirically within discursive and institutional complexes, and it is employed in a quasi-transcendental manner as a condition of possibility for the human sciences. It should make possible a structurally oriented genealogical analysis of the descent of historically established institutions, forms of knowledge, and, in general, the technologies of power that constitute the apparent facticity of all social objects. Power practices entail the dimension of shifting power relations, which can be located through the analysis of emergence but nonetheless cannot be formalized. These practices should, by using the dynamics of struggle, secure a systematic place for the pragmatic aspect of the historical a priori which, in the archaeological conceptual scheme, remained entangled in irresolvable aporias. The fact that this second concept of power is not explicitly thematized in Foucault's major studies of descent can be explained as resulting from its character as a fluid, non-formalizable background, which bars its systematic observation.

Clearly the reconstruction of Foucault's concept of power just suggested will sooner defer than resolve the difficulties posed by his earlier theoretical endeavors. Now as ever, the problem of the performative contradiction arises: Foucault cannot apply genealogy to his own theory. Despite the doubled articulation of the concept of power, he is still faced with the question found in *The Archaeology of Knowledge*; that is, he cannot account for the question of the pragmatic, empirico-transcendental character of power practices, practices which cannot be defined and yet, nonetheless, play a key role in the architectonics of his theory.

What the doubled model of power brings to light, however, is that Foucault's intuition of a presubjective a priori endures. In its articulation as the will to knowledge and as power practices, it even more explicitly calls to mind the idea of Bachelard's scientific spirit. Namely, if one freed Bachelard's philosophy from its psychologistic aspects, that is to say, those deriving from a philosophy of the subject which Foucault—influenced as he is by the idea of the end of the individual—does not share, then the motif of a doubled, both structural and creative, transcendental would remain as their common matrix. For both authors, this transcendental takes on new forms and constitutes new objects of experience in the course of its historical transformations.

The fact that Foucault expands the spectrum of constituted objects from the scientific to the social, including the individual, does not change the basic figure of thought: that of an anonymous structuring a priori (for Bachelard, a mathematical a priori that operates on the level of the natural sciences; for Foucault, a will to knowledge that operates on the social level and that advances processes of individuation) that is driven to change forms or historical constellations by the creative force of a pre-individualistic, innovative spirit (Bachelard) or a pulsating network of power practices (Foucault).

Chapter Five

An Overview

The endeavor carried out thus far, to examine the various periods of Foucault's intellectual development by hermeneutically privileging the influence of several Bachelardian motifs, would not be very helpful if no new elements were furnished thereby that could clear up apparent contradictions, offer new critical perspectives, or even make possible an entirely new picture of the intuitions and expressive force of Foucault's theory.

With this in mind, I would now like to use some of the results of my epistemological reading of Foucault to advance some theses regarding the most mature and impressive expression of Foucault's thought, the theory of power.

In many respects, the recently published studies on antiquity[1] constitute a completely different topic. For this reason, I will address them in a more cursory manner later on. Their open-ended character and the disparity between them and the earlier writings are so striking that they, to my mind, allow me to make my concluding comments with regard to the theory of power at this time.

The Struggle for Objectification

My first remark concerns the concept of power.

> Who wages war against whom? Is it between two
> classes, or more? Is it a war of all against all? . . . What
> is the relevance of concepts of tactics and strategy for
> analyzing structures and political processes? What is
> the essence and mode of transformation of power rela-
> tions? All these questions need to be explored.[2]

Foucault does not explicitly answer the question of what
is at stake with power. For all that, it is clear that his conception of power comprises a critique of Marxist economics.
In many places Foucault characterizes Marxism in an ad
hoc manner and then argues vehemently for the by now
mundane insight that economic interest is an insufficient
category for understanding the mechanisms of power in
developed societies. Historically, Foucault's renunciation
of the economic model as a way to explain the emergence of
capitalist society was coupled with the theses from
Discipline and Punish, which attributed authorship for the
conditions necessary for the emergence of capitalism to the
disciplinary and individuating processes produced by the
will to knowledge. Seen in terms of a theory of society,
power, or biopower, should constitute the horizon against
which all social manifestations can be explained adequately.
This line of questioning, which promises so much, makes
an answer even more necessary—if not a substantialist
answer regarding the nature of power, then at least an
answer regarding its role within a theory of society. The
interpretive strategy that emerges from an epistemologically oriented reading of Foucault is one that transposes the
epistemological problematic of the earlier writings into a
theory of society in the form of a general *struggle for reciprocal objectification* between social actors.

If the two moments of power, that is, the will to knowledge and power practices, are examined together, it can be
seen that power as a whole cannot be conceptualized on

the model of pure mastery and violence. The concept of apparatus clarifies how the two moments of power become one unitary complex. Although the utilization of brute force within an apparatus is possible, it does not represent the decisive feature of the exercise of power. If one wants to describe a power complex, the example of the functioning of an apparatus, such as the panopticon, works particularly well. Here, normative moments and technical equipment converge, becoming a kind of structural force.[3] These elements do not have physical martyrdom as their goal, as Foucault shows by comparing them to the disciplinary rituals of the Classical period; rather, they are characterized by a refined technology of "docile bodies."

To my mind, the goal of the power typical of prisons, schools, barracks, and the army can best be conceptualized on the model of a struggle for objectification because it does justice to all the features of power. According to this model, the strategic confrontation between individuals finds both its means and its ends in the will to knowledge. This explains, among other things, why it was so difficult for Foucault to describe the purpose of these struggles. This description is so difficult because the goal is tantamount to the effects that are produced in the struggle.

Foucault describes a kind of distorted struggle for recognition in which there can be neither reconciliation nor resolution in the form of victory for one of the parties, such as is achieved when a disputed object is secured. For, in this struggle, processes of objectification and individuation represent both the proceedings necessary for the exercise of power and its never completely attainable goal. They thereby repeat the aporetic schema of the human sciences. Here, as in the human sciences, what is central is the idea of a self-referentiality that is brought about in the realistic attitude of traditional epistemology and which, due to its false premises, is enmeshed in a hopeless tangle. At the same time society is thought of as a macro-subject that bears the mark of the will to knowledge; within this structure individuals are seen as both the objects and the bearers of its constitutive practice. What was described in the discussion of the human sciences as the *internal* aporetic process of an epistemological constellation of knowledge is presented in *Discipline and Punish* in the *external* form of a self-referential social relation produced by the external mediation of its actors. The guard from the inner tower of the panopticon acts as part of the prison's surveillance apparatus and thus belongs to the machinery that coproduces processes of individuation via the constitutive role of technology. According to the interpretive model I have suggested, however, the guard can be thought to be just as much the object or the product of the machinery of constitution that produced and repeatedly secures and strengthens his individuation as the prisoners are, even though he is subject to other apparatuses (family, school, army, even work relations). On this basis, one can try to answer the question regarding the object of power practices on the micro-level, via the idea of a societal circulation of objectification or individuation processes that obey the universal law of Western societies: the will to knowledge.

This heuristic model has the advantage of taking many aspects of Foucault's theory of power into account. It is able to systematize, in their declared context of a "common history of power relations and knowledge relations," both the pair will to knowledge/micrological power practices as well as, on the methodological level, the pair analysis of descent/analysis of emergence. In this "common history" the quasi-transcendental and the empirical moments found both in the will to knowledge and in power practices merge at the level of the individual in the continuum of circular, reciprocal objectification. In addition, Foucault's specific, holistic intuition[4] is retained in this model of the struggle for objectification, despite any intrinsic implausibility. That is, the intuition of an uncentered whole is retained, within which context and rules can be articulated with regard to their function, but no longer with regard to categorial distinctions. Rather, they are anchored in provisional constellations of rules. This occurs in such a way that, in keeping with Foucault's theory, the hermeneutic dimension of every-day social life is diminished. By conceptualizing society as a practical network of objectification, hermeneutic under-standing and its communicative-theoretic presuppositions,[5] as well as systems of norms anchored in the lifeworld, are replaced by the idea of a complex that stands under the ban-ner of the will to knowledge. In it each actor is simultane-ously the object and the agent of mute processes of individ-uation. Since practices are subsumed under the epistemological motif of the will to knowledge, social prac-tice is ultimately reduced to a mere disciplinary and, at the same time, constitutive relation in which the actions of indi-viduals seemingly repeat the aporetic structure of the human sciences by carrying out the fate of "man and his doubles."[6]

Such a conceptualization of power leaves at least two questions unanswered. First of all, there is the problem of the individual, who emerges as a passive figure in *Discipline and Punish*, taking the form of either the mere object of normative institutions or as their docile agent. This reduc-tion of intersubjective relations to reciprocal forms of objec-tification is questionable not only from a perspective exter-nal to Foucault's theory, but also with regard to Foucault's own claim to derive something like the emergence of inwardness or the "soul" from his theory. Secondly—and related to the problem of the individual—is the question regarding the sources of his critique and, if applicable, regarding his analysis of the forces that could embody a crit-ical moment within the social context. This question is also raised by Foucault's own perspective, which carries out its analysis of power with an unmistakable critical intent and which raises with new urgency and in a new form the problem already brought up by his early writings: that of the systematic place of his critique.

New Subjects of Struggles

Foucault carries out some correctives in the first vol-ume of *The History of Sexuality* that, in end effect, grant individual subjectivity a greater theoretical relevance for social practice. Foucault analyzes sexuality as a historical complex produced by refined techniques of control, tracing its development from confession up until psychoanalysis. Through this approach, Foucault discloses an aspect of individuation through which the direct disciplinary interventions of power onto the body assume the more subtle form of a disciplinary introspection. The subject now actively disciplines him or herself, appropriating, as it were, the mechanism of control found in the will to knowledge and using it against him or herself. "An imperative was established: Not only will you confess to acts contravening the law, but you will seek to transform your desire, your every desire, into discourse."[7] Despite the change of topic to sexuality, the theme and the object of criticism remain the same. The supposedly deep introspection practiced today by the most sophisticated form of psychoanalysis, with the promise that it will free the individual's innermost and hidden motivations, is a dangerous lie. Rather than restoring a suppressed freedom, it allows a more subtle form of social control to take hold. Indeed, by assuming that a hidden human substance can be found in sexuality, it merely embodies a more subtle form of the will to knowledge.

> If sexuality was constituted as an area of investigation, this was only because relations of power had established it as a possible object; and conversely, if power was able to take it as a target, this was because techniques of knowledge and procedures of discourse were capable of investing it.[8]

Although Foucault's analysis, even here, stays within the theoretical framework of his writings on power, by attributing more active and fully articulated intrinsic capacities to the individual a change is initiated that will have far-reaching effects on his later writings. This change was probably also brought about by systematic internal and external pressures to make explicit within his theory the practicable emancipatory perspective that was always among Foucault's motivations.

In 1976, the year that *The History of Sexuality* was first published, Foucault sketched out in an interview an interesting role for the intellectual.[9] He condemns as trite the figure of the universal intellectual, that is, the intellectual who, in the paradigmatic role of the author, acts as the protector of a universality that is advocated by other social groups only in an impure form. Counter to this view, Foucault advocates the idea of the "specific" intellectual, claiming it is an appropriate designation for the forces that represent a critical, or better said, a subversive potential in normalized society.

> Intellectuals have got used to working, not in the modality of the "universal," the "exemplary," the "just-and-true-for-all," but within specific sectors, at the precise points where their own conditions of life or work situate them (housing, the hospital, the asylum, the laboratory, the university, family and sexual relations). This has undoubtedly given them a much more immediate and concrete awareness of struggles. And they have met here with problems which are specific, "non-universal."[10]

Using his impressive sensibility for diagnosing his times, Foucault's analysis undoubtedly does note actual and relevant changes in the critical mindset that emerged in the years after the student revolts. Anti-psychiatry, anti-technocratic orientations in all scientific areas, as well as grassroots movements, the women's movement, prisoners' protests, and the new self-confidence of homosexuals, confirm the picture of a society in which critical knowledge and action emerge from various, diffuse work and life relations, are each processed in a specific manner, and then are employed in innumerable micro-struggles. His diagnosis of the decline of the figure of the intellectual, symbolized by the writer, has its own plausibility as well, insofar as it notes the end of a strategic role for the critique of ideology in an ever more rationalized lifeworld, a lifeworld that no longer produces the conditions necessary for ideologies to operate in their traditional manner.[11]

How compatible is the critical perspective associated with the specific intellectual with the model of the social struggle for objectification introduced earlier, which was characterized by its explicit exclusion of any normative dimension?

Hidden Normativity

The idea of the specific intellectual is not an isolated phenomenon. Rather, it is part of a series of indicators that, around the year 1976, signals Foucault's increased preoccupation with the problem of an instance that is critical of, or not in conformity with, power. The "pleasures" that are briefly mentioned in connection with the hypothetical conception of "a different economy of bodies and pleasures"[12] in the first volume of *The History of Sexuality* seem to reveal the bare outlines of a utopian perspective. This hypothetical perspective is supplemented by a diagnosis, completely new for Foucault, of instances that can ultimately be called subversive moments within the existing order of power. Foucault speaks of an "insurrection of subjugated knowledges";[13] these knowledges lack the requisite qualifications and thus are not socially recognized. It is the knowledge of "the psychiatric patient, of the ill person, of the nurse, of the doctor—parallel and marginal as they are to the knowledge of medicine—that of the delinquent etc. . . ."[14] that Foucault designates as "popular knowledge." This knowledge represents the always situated source, as it were, from which the specific intellectual procures the contents of his critical engagement.

These indicators make an important addition to the model I have suggested, which interprets power within society in terms of a generalized struggle for objectification. The utopian reliance on pleasures to counter normalizing sexual science, the adoption of a critical role for the specific intellectual, and the related thesis regarding the insurrection of subjugated knowledges, suggest that the practices of individual actors do not necessarily have to take place under the objectifying force of the will to knowledge. At the very least, these practices can be said to lack an objectifying character, otherwise their nonconformity to power could not be accounted for. If we then try to move from a merely negative to a positive definition of such critical occurrences, which amounts to trying to uncover the hidden normative premises[15] that are admitted by Foucault's conceptualization of critical occurrences, then we must turn to the implicit normative dimension of his epistemology because it offers the only plausible solution to this problem. Thus far we have seen that Foucault—in the period concerned with power as well—rejects every anthropologically oriented justification of power and power practices for reasons made known in his critique of the human sciences. It has also been shown that the idea of an "other" of power, after some ambivalence in his early writings, finally disappears for good from his sphere of thought.[16] As a result, his early writings are unable to provide the key that would allow either an anthropological or an irrational approach to develop a relevant normative principle that would be critical of power. Since Foucault's theory of society lacks a communicative basis, the only remaining hypothesis is that the normative basis of his critique should be sought in a figure of thought similar to that found in Bachelard's historical epistemology.

It has been shown that Bachelard's skepticism vis-à-vis the foundations of the sciences follows from his view that scientific theory formation is a creative act of construction that has apodeictic value. Scientific progress is not secured by the methodic development of a language of observation but by the constructions themselves which, by increasing the amount of evidence, make themselves ever more plausible and, in a certain sense, better founded. It was also shown that the creative activity of spirit, above and beyond its role of providing the criterion for scientific progress, was raised to the rank of the universal principle guiding a scientific-ascetic way of life. Thus, it was claimed that scientific productivity is not an instrument used to manipulate external nature; it is not in the service of an everyday life whose moral and theoretical significance is misjudged from the very start. Rather, scientific productivity (along with poetry) is declared to be the only life goal worth striving for.[17]

Indeed, throughout this investigation I have repeatedly acknowledged the motif of creative productivity in my attempts to reconstruct the character of the historical a priori in the different periods of Foucault's thought. Even power practices were interpreted, in light of this characteristic, as an empirico-transcendental complex that comprises the actions of individuals as well as the historico-epistemological structure of the will to knowledge. This characterization of the aforementioned complex led to the definition of social struggles as being concerned with objectification. Now, by turning to the normative significance of creativity for Bachelard, we can try to explain the normative meaning behind the forms of resistance to power that are introduced by Foucault with his formulations of the specific individual and the insurrection of subjugated knowledges. Consulting Foucault himself, we read that subjugated knowledges are those that "have been disqualified as inadequate to their task or insufficiently elaborated: naive knowledges, located low down on the hierarchy, beneath the required level of cognition or scientificity."[18] One can make Foucault's definition even more explicit by adding that the requisite level of cognition or scientificity that disqualifies such knowledges ultimately can be determined by no other criterion than this: whether these knowledges can be included in the constellation of the objectifying and self-referential human sciences characteristic of the will to knowledge, or whether they must be excluded for not conforming to the human sciences' compulsion towards objectification.

As a matter of fact, Foucault does not need to appeal to instances that are somehow external to his theory of power in order to carry out such a critique of power. Rather, he only needs to extricate the creative dimension that has always belonged to his concept of power practices due to its ties to the historical constellation of the will to knowledge. It has been shown that the power-knowledge apparatus, be it in prison, in school, in the barracks, but also in the family and in the more subtle self-reflective practices addressed in the first volume of *The History of Sexuality*, which range from confession to psychoanalysis, conforms to power to the degree that it induces the normalizing attribution of social identity from the outside in the processes of objectification it compels. And it has been shown that the objectifying effect of these practices is only possible because the epistemological structure of the will to knowledge operates on the basis of the realistic fallacy, which occasions the neverending, and for disciplinary instances crucial search for a substance, and which brings about the resulting proliferation in the production of ever more profound tendencies towards objectification and subjectification.

Foucault's strategy can be reconstructed with Bachelard's normative premises such that it runs counter to *this* power, perverted into the form of the will to knowledge, which transforms its creativity to serve normalization in the empty productivity of the human sciences. Namely, his thought can be reconstructed in terms of a creative subjectivity that is no longer solely attributed to the scientist but to every social actor and that first unfolds when it is freed from traditional epistemology's fixation on the object (Bachelard) or the will to knowledge (Foucault).

Viewed from this epistemological perspective, social groups seem more or less like scientific collectives who try to assert their own situated, contextual knowledge by securing its social validity. Like Bachelard's interregional rationalism,[19] where the autonomous disciplines of the sciences only produce a special and local knowledge, the creative knowledge of resistance also presents itself in a regional manner. Resistance represents a "particular, local, regional knowledge, a differential knowledge incapable of unanimity."[20] Foucault stresses that the main concern here is not "popular knowledge." What makes resistance possible for social groups, in Foucault's analysis, is a "historical knowledge of struggles." This knowledge emerges from the collective memory of groups of subjects who have been objectified, or rather, individuated, by disciplinary practices and by the manipulations they have suffered; the erudition of the specific intellectual is of assistance in unearthing it and keeping it alive.

At approximately this point in Foucault's model the universal intellectual is replaced by the specific intellectual, who may take the form of an individual or group. For the specific intellectual, whose creative self-representation breaks through the objectification and ascription of identity imposed by the will to knowledge and who asserts a new style and a new view of himself or herself, best expresses Foucault's hidden normative conception, which was inspired by Bachelard's epistemology. For Bachelard, the virtue of scientific genius lay in liberating oneself from passively assimilated views that falsely depicted external nature as something given and in producing new scientific objects via the creative act of theory formation. Similarly, in Foucault's model of society it is the creativity of social actors that provides the criterion whereby the productivity of normalizing and objectifying actions governed by the will to knowledge is to be distinguished from those actions that resist it. By examining these normative premises we will be able to see what is at stake with the practice of "resistance" in Foucault's conception of society: It is a matter of asserting the social validity of a *self-produced* identity (self-produced mainly by groups but also by individuals) in opposition to the compulsion, exercised by the will to knowledge via its various disciplinary and social scientific moments, towards assuming forms of identity sanctioned by dominant social values. Thus the struggles of the mad, prisoners, homosexuals, and women consist in establishing their own style, their own social image vis-à-vis other social groups and contrary to dominant psychiatric, penal, and sexist roles.

Foucault's "Applied Rationalism"

On the one hand, the passive bearers of the processes of objectification; on the other, the subjects of creative self-representations who revolt against the objectification imposed upon them. All of this is dispersed across innumerable micro-struggles in which each, according to context and role, is either an agent of normalization or a subject resisting objectification.

There are substantive and methodical implications to this reconstruction of the normative premises behind Foucault's view of society. Acting subjects who devise forms of resistance out of their work and life contexts, reinvigorate a historical knowledge of earlier struggles, and perhaps even adopt a utopian attitude and aim at a "new economy of bodies and pleasures," can be accommodated neither by the old conceptualization of the mere functions of discourses, nor by the more recent theory of power, which attributes to these subjects only the role of strategically equipped bearers of power practices. Foucault says:

> When one defines the exercise of power as a mode of action upon the actions of others, when one characterizes these actions by the government of men by other men—in the broadest sense of the term—one includes an important element: freedom. Power is exercised only over free subjects, and only insofar as they are free.[22]

This is the almost inevitable result of Foucault's gradual abandonment of structuralism, a theory which characterized his thought from the time of his failed attempt at semiological analysis in *The Archaeology of Knowledge* up until his final writings on antiquity. The more decisively he distances himself from the structuralist topos of the "end of the individual," the more urgent it becomes to reach a theoretical determination of the rediscovered concept of the individual. Foucault does not say what systematic role will be played by the freedom he mentions; it is possible, however, to advance a hypothesis that is in agreement with the normative premises described above. The line of questioning associated there with the theory of society converges with the methodological premises of Foucault's analysis since he, by raising substantive questions about social actors, can now discuss the problem of his own situatedness as a part of the object under investigation.

What was impossible in the semiological period, the self-thematization of the archaeologist with regard to the theory of signs, can now be undertaken anew in the context of a theory of power which integrates the motif of an anonymous historical a priori with the power practices carried out by (free) subjects. Thus, Foucault can understand himself and his work as both the result of, and the interpreter of, a historical constellation of power; the detachment of the archaeologist is supplemented by the partial analysis of a participant involved in the struggle. In this context Dreyfus and Rabinow define Foucault's new method as "interpretive analytics";[23] it is a combination of archaeology and genealogy that supplements the detached observation of discursive formations with an interpretation of the practices that underlie discourse and include the interpreter himself or herself. The subject of such an interpretive analytic is thought to be free, as is every social subject who derives interpretations, analyses, and plans for action from the particular constellation of his or her life relations. This methodological attitude does not imply, however, that Foucault has adopted the hermeneutic approach. Dreyfus and Rabinow write with regard to this:

> The resulting interpretation is a pragmatically guided reading of the coherence of the practices of the society. It does not claim to correspond either to the everyday meanings shared by the actors or, in any simple sense, to reveal the intrinsic meaning of the practices. This is the sense in which Foucault's method is interpretive but not hermeneutic.[24]

According to Foucault's particular formulation, interpretation should not reveal a profound meaning that is hidden in the text; rather, it should make comprehensible the context in which the subject is located so that it can be changed.[25] Foucault explicates his conception of interpretation as follows:

> But if interpretation is the violent or surreptitious appropriation of a system of rules, which in itself has no essential meaning, in order to impose a direction . . . then the development of humanity is a series of interpretations.[26]

The meaning and terminology found in Foucault's concept of interpretation obviously come from Nietzsche's genealogy. The emphasis on the relational character of the objects of interpretation also stems from Nietzsche.

A further explanation of the particular meaning of an "appropriation of a system of rules with no essential meaning" can be attempted here as well by comparing Foucault's concept of interpretation with Bachelard's concept of construction. Certainly the concept of construction, which Bachelard applies to his model of how scientists relate to mathematics, is not immediately relevant to "appropriating" rules, as Foucault calls it (although Bachelard frequently uses formulations that suggest the relation to Nietzschean motifs).[27] But in spite of this the fundamental similarity between the two procedures can be easily ascertained. Both scientific construction and the interpretive achievements of the genealogist begin with relations, because both procedures want to avoid the substantialist fallacy and because both have, not the knowledge of, but rather the production of scientific and social objects as their goal. Furthermore, Bachelard's construction as well as Foucault's interpretation renounce the formation of a knowledge that is rooted in the lifeworld, and they understand the reference to relation as characteristic of an activity that owes its production of knowledge to the abstractness of its relations. Along these lines Foucault writes that genealogy is concerned with a differentiated "regional" knowledge that is formed in contrast to what is seen as the "normalized" knowledge of everyday life. Scientific construction and genealogical interpretation emerge neither from subjective motivations nor from "materially" based interests. Rather, they emerge by creatively appropriating abstract systems of rules—that is, they emerge out of a creativity that, both for Bachelard and Foucault, is the main characteristic of a science that is liberated from the aporetic striving for foundations of the will to truth (be it in Bachelard's original epistemological form or in that of the human sciences or of a normalizing power).

The comparison that has been outlined here between Bachelard's construction and Foucault's concept of interpretation can serve the end of examining and criticizing the distinctive aspects of Foucault's ideal of scientific procedure. There can be no doubt about Foucault's "positivism." Even in the period concerned with power, that is, after his explicit preoccupation with epistemological themes fell aside with *The Archaeology of Knowledge*, Foucault insists on characterizing genealogy as "anti-science," not in the sense of a "lyrical right to ignorance or non-knowledge"[28] but as a completely rational undertaking.

> Let us give the term *genealogy* to the union of erudite knowledge and local memories which allows us to establish a historical knowledge of struggles and to make use of this knowledge tactically today.[29]

According to his own self-understanding, Foucault in fact held that both his writing of history and the beginnings of a theory of society that accompanied it were a rational matter. However, he also held that they obtained their distinctiveness and its superiority vis-à-vis the conventional human sciences from the fact that they lacked the objectifying character of the will to knowledge or of the will to truth.

One could say in closing that this particular kind of interpretation (named "interpretive analytics" by Dreyfus and Rabinow), which amounts to the ability to consider rel-

evant or structural features of one's own society and to com-
bine them in new forms, is analogous to Bachelard's concept
of construction even in its most conspicuous weakness: its
hopeless indeterminacy.

Just as Bachelard believed that scientific construction
could account for everything from historical reconstructions, to psychoanalytically oriented observations, all the
way to the intersubjective understanding of the scientific
community,[30] so is Foucault's interpretation little more than
an empty designation that does not allow important theoretical distinctions to be made. In describing the critical
role of the intellectual or of social actors in reappropriating
historical struggles through the use of memory, Foucault
refers to functional achievements that could be analyzed, for
example, in terms of communicative theory. When these
achievements are lumped together under the catchword
"interpretation" or "genealogy," however, they lose all theoretical relevance.

This problem is raised even more clearly when Foucault
the genealogist derives the validity and the systematic position of his own work from his own historical context. By
conceding his involvement in the investigated object and
by putting himself in the position of all other social actors,
Foucault at least remedied the most flagrant manifestations
of his lack of self-thematization, which was the most conspicuous aporia of his theory from the earliest writings up
until *The Archaeology of Knowledge*. Consistently applying
genealogy to one's own situation as a theorist, however,
unavoidably results in the drastic relativization of the truth
content of one's own theory. Foucault is consistent.
Namely, in numerous interviews he stresses that everything he has written is concerned with producing "effects,"
not true theses.[31] Foucault is in agreement with Bachelard's
theses here as well in that he underlines the superiority of
the applied production of knowledge as compared to the
sterility of a search for truth that, for him, belonged to the
sphere of traditional epistemology anyway. He even goes
further than Bachelard, radicalizing this insight by enter-

ing the theoretical laboratory himself as the producer of new cultural syntheses and directly experimenting on the production of various possible sociocultural effects. Thereby, however, his anti-science is reduced to the level of a mere application of technology, and his theory is reduced to a "politics of theory."[32]

A Technology of Liberation?

The fact that Foucault's writings have significant import for a politics of theory should not be allowed to obscure their considerable effect on the contemporary philosophical discussion. Foucault could serve as an exemplar of the partial truth that historians of science, like Feyerabend,[33] express when they see the success of a theory as tied to its favorable convergence with conditions external to science. Namely, viewed "externally" Foucault's new concepts, his "effects," had the good fortune of coinciding with certain cultural expectations that characterized the unease and the experiences of a large part of an entire generation after the student revolts of 1968. In my view, the possibility of creatively working through this unease is the decisive motif that made Foucault's theory, apart from questions of its intrinsic consistency, so effective, even in the philosophic sphere. Habermas diagnoses this theory as suffering from "syndromes of reneging on the left."[34] These syndromes appear promptly after the failure of revolutions or revolts, dissolving their universalistic content as well as their tools for cultural enlightenment, for having acted on behalf of the "terror of reason." Undoubtedly this thesis expresses the central point of Foucault's position. Its details, however, can be filled in by considering other aspects. For instance, Foucault presents a series of functional equivalents, as it were, for the topoi of the Marxist tradition which, even after 1968, continued to serve as the theoretical framework for many intellectuals even though their "Marxism" was no longer compatible with orthodox

Marxist teaching. Foucault's pathos for a critique of ideology seems to be related to the Marxist tradition as well, even though his critique of ideology no longer is one but rather has been transformed into a genealogical critique of reason. Equally kindred to the Marxist tradition is the peculiar positivism of an anti-science that is meant to be a critique of other sciences and that, in addition, should provide the key to understanding the conditions necessary for the emergence of a society that hinders the free unfolding of humanity. Above all, however, this theory is suited to bring to the fore romantic modernist themes, which were present throughout the Marxist tradition and were especially pronounced in the student movements, and to supplement them with a critique of culture.

It may not be a coincidence that so-called "postmodern" theorists, of whom Foucault is a prominent representative, come from the French philosophical tradition. Namely, there more than elsewhere the emancipatory motives of the student revolts were very quickly and decisively turned into the cadre-activism of Marxist-Leninist organizations. When the attempts at revolution failed along with their avant-garde certitudes, the critique of culture which had been sacrificed on the altar of revolutionary politics was found to offer too narrow a basis to support social movements with the strength of the Federal Republic of Germany or the United States.

Against this background Foucault's theory could appear as an instrument that promises to lend a new theoretical consistency to the aesthetic-expressive and culture-critical themes of the student revolts. Thereby it enriches the spectrum of counter-enlightenment positions by adding a "leftist" and thus a particularly interesting variant. The fascination of Foucault consists precisely in the fact that he holds out the prospect of a "technology of liberation," as I would like to call it, that is neither technocratic nor moralistic. His genealogy, with its struggle of social subjects against objectification, offers an anti-science that is anti-technocratic for the reason that it can be practiced only when it unites "erudition with the memory of past struggles" against the forces of normalization. In addition, this theory can replace the moralism of a revolutionary eschatology with a notion of liberation that does not demand sacrificial victims in order to reach a substantive utopia, but rather elicits its contents from the specific experience and the subversive practice of an actor or a collective. The technology of liberation is not presented as an irrational retreat in the strict sense of the term because its applied character promises analytical tools for political orientation. And it is not merely a theory without norms because its critique of humanism should smooth the way to the real liberation of every individual on the basis of his or her respective needs for self-realization or self-determination. In my view it is these "external" motifs which, even when filtered through the academic lens, explain in part the relevance of Foucault's theory.

But a theory that claims to be both social analysis and, in a certain sense, "critical theory"[35] commits a serious mistake if it only sees critical potential in social actors' aesthetic-expressive moments. The conceptualization of society as a struggle against objectification and for self-representation, criticized above,[36] as well as the neglect of the normative basis that ensures a society's cohesion, are consistently reflected in the conspicuous one-sidedness of the possible forms of emancipation proposed by Foucault. The technology of liberation relies on an increasing awareness on the part of social actors that they can take their own subject formation in hand, rather than submitting to the normalizing processes of individuation. Individuals

> assert the right to be different and they underline everything which makes individuals truly individual. On the other hand, they attack everything which separates the individual, breaks his links with others, splits up community life, forces the individual back on himself and ties him to his own identity in a constraining way.[37]

Foucault makes these "struggles against the government of individuation" central to his analysis and hails them here for emphasizing a liberatory perspective; they presuppose a conception of processes of individuation, however, that completely ignores the element of socialization. Mead's insight, that is, that individuation is to be viewed as an aspect of processes of socialization[38] and that a continuum exists between the sphere of inwardness and the communicative structures of the lifeworld, falls outside the horizon of Foucault's thought. As a result, in his view of society the emancipatory perspective of autonomous individuation is robbed of the element of a parallel progressive universalization in interpersonal relations. The weakness of his social analysis, which fails to designate a place for the communicative structures of social life, is repeated in the idea of an emancipation that cannot take into account moral-practical learning processes in addition to an aesthetic-expressive conception of individuation.

The Aesthetics of Existence

The most surprising and probably most radical turn in Foucault's thought takes place in volumes 2 and 3 of *The History of Sexuality*.[39] Even more strongly than in the transition from *Madness and Civilization* to the semiological writings or from these to the theory of power, one is confronted with an entirely different project. This investigation of Greco-Roman antiquity, a highly unusual object domain for a specialist of the seventeenth and eighteenth centuries, already marks the thematic distance from the earlier and otherwise relatively homogenous studies. Foucault's style is transformed as well; instead of the rhetorically extremely adroit, in some cases positively baroque mode of presentation, one finds a straightforward and clearly developed prose. The most important differences are to be found primarily in the theoretical approach, however. Foucault investigates the birth and development of inwardness in the beginnings of Western culture, in ancient Greece. The task thereby is no longer to expose the discontinuity of events that lies behind the appearance of continuity provided by human history; rather, it is to examine progress in the process of the formation of subjectivity, despite historical turning points, such as the transition from the Hellenistic to the Christian age.

Thus, Foucault is no longer the thinker of discontinuity. But as far back as the theory of power and then especially since the "History of Problematizations," which are characteristic of volumes 2 and 3 of *The History of Sexuality*, Foucault can no longer be said to be the thinker of the "end of the individual" either. The two correctives to his course are related. The prophecy of the disappearance of the person, "like a face drawn in the sand at the edge of the sea," is only possible if one assumes that history consists of a series of *epistemes* and is subordinate to their discontinuous dissolution. As we have seen, over the years the structuralist character of Foucault's work has diminished, particularly as a result of the systematic shift in emphasis which has forced him to a preoccupation with the problem of the individual.

By dating back the time of the individual's first appearance and at the same time weakening the motif of an anonymous historical a priori, Foucault can make his concept of the individual more plausible. In Foucault's rigid schema of a series of *epistemes* (*The Order of Things*), the problematic of the individual is limited to the margins of the modern concern with the doubled empirico-transcendental self of the human sciences. A more complex analysis of the individual first becomes possible for Foucault when, with the introduction of the concept of power at the beginning of the 1970s[40] (in the first volume of *The History of Sexuality* and in some minor writings), a reinterpretation of the historical a priori occurs which replaces the abrupt transition of "incommensurable" *epistemes* with the micro-discontinuities of numerous power practices. As a result, critical junctures in the historical process become so fragmented and widely dispersed, indeed ultimately drained of drama, that they, too, can be thought of as a kind of unstable continuum. Thus, despite epochal change, once again it becomes systematically possible for a thematic complex to endure over longer time spans.

The culmination of this change occurs in volumes 2 and 3 of *The History of Sexuality*. In these texts the solution to a dilemma starts to emerge—a dilemma that was implicit in the problem of the individual in Foucault's final writings on power. Specifically, Foucault either stands by his idea of the suprasubjective historical a priori that characterized all of his previous writings in order to maintain the coherence of his theory, even though this is incompatible with his description of individual agents as autonomously acting subjects—or he pursues the logic of his new insights regarding the individual; completes the process he has already embarked upon, of revising his anti-subjectivism; and thereby undermines the basic intuition of an anonymous historical a priori. Foucault is too intellectually open and curious to undergo self-censorship for systematic reasons. Naturally he chooses the latter possibility; he lets himself be carried along by a growing interest in the individuality problematic, and he finally sacrifices the continuity of his approach to his fascination with the object of his analysis:

> As for what motivated me, it is quite simple; I would hope that in the eyes of some it might be sufficient in itself. It was curiosity—the only kind of curiosity, in any case, that is worth acting upon with a degree of obstinacy: . . . that which enables one to get free of oneself.[41]

Admittedly, the terminology of the earlier writings does not disappear from *The Uses of Pleasure*, especially not from the introduction. Foucault still discusses archaeology and genealogy and practices within the framework of a history of truth,[42] but the sphere of application of these concepts is so altered that they ultimately cannot hide their change in meaning. For neither forms of knowledge nor power formations stand in the center of this theory now; individuals do.[43] In many places Foucault points to a kind of stratification of his studies such that his investigation of subject formation in Western culture could be thought of as supplementing his archaeological and genealogical works. However, the main idea of his final books—a history of the "problematizations"[44] of sexual pleasures by way of practices of the self which bring "into play the criteria of an 'aesthetic of existence'"[45]—seem to be light years away from *epistemes* and apparatuses, from statements and bodies. Foucault writes that after the analysis of knowledge and power, analysis of the subject has central importance. But the impact of his analysis of knowledge and power stemmed from its refusal to view the "subject" as a possible object domain for archaeology or genealogy and from its description of subjects as "effects" of the power/knowledge complex, that is, as the results of anonymous relations.[46] It is the omission of this point that deprives Foucault's work of its center and allows a radically other theory to appear. The archaeology of problematizations and the genealogy of the self[47] are no longer fundamentally different from the usual "humanist" writings of history.

Even more interesting than such breaks, however, are the aspects of continuity that unfold despite, or better yet, because of, the above-mentioned breaks. The latter can be found in the critique of normalizing (self-) objectification. I have repeatedly shown in these pages that this motif is developed in all the periods of Foucault's theory: In the critique of psychology and psychiatry, in the contradictions of the human sciences, and in the disciplinary function of the will to knowledge. It has been shown that the thematic area out of which this critique of objectification arose bears many similarities to Bachelard's critique of realism and is marked by the same opposition between substantialism and creativity.[48] In Foucault's studies of antiquity it is even clearer how fundamental this figure of thought is because here it is free of all structuralist demands. Foucault describes how pleasures were problematized through practices of the self in antiquity and how these problematizations first led to the Stoic ideal of an aesthetic of existence and later led to Christian practices of self-scrutiny. By contrasting these two ways of thinking, indeed, traditions of thought, all the systematic pairs found in the course of Foucault's thought, such as the human sciences/*episteme* or the will to knowledge/power practices, obtain a form that has historical content as well as, finally, an explicit normative basis.

In a kind of philosophical confession, Foucault names the normative idea that was hidden behind the concepts of dream, madness, *epistemes*, and power and that indeed, was perhaps even misunderstood by him: that is, an aesthetic of self-representation as the ethical alternative to Christian introspection. If one analyzes Foucault's theory retrospectively, in light of his final writings, it seems to be more of a romantic positivism rather than a felicitous one. His critique of Christian morality, which leaves its stamp on Western culture to the present day, is positivist in the broadest sense of the term. For Christian morality, which is based on universal commands, is not criticized by means of a moral-practical discourse, but rather because, in Foucault's eyes, its consequences are simply epistemologically wrong. The mistake made by Christian morality—its doubling of the world, its distinction between the purity of universal commands and the imperfection of empirical ones—is epistemological, because it presupposes that the person has a pure substance that can be separated from the base inclinations of empirical life. According to Foucault, the absurd practices of self-scrutiny, of introspection in the hope of purifying the self and liberating what is actually substantial from everything that is inessential, result from this error. In Foucault's theory Bachelard's critique of substantialist epistemology is extended into a critique of morality that more or less unites all the motifs of his thought into one extreme, synthetic form. A substantialist conception of morality stretches from Plato to the "California culture of introspection"; it rests on false epistemological assumptions and can be unmasked via genealogy.

The romantic Foucault is just as much in evidence in his final writings. What was described in the earlier stages of Foucault's thought as the motif of a creative, pre-individualistic subjectivity that could be located in the categories of the dream, madness, *episteme*, discourse, or power, now takes the form of the practice of subjects who creatively and harmoniously reform the given spheres of life. The aesthetic of existence, that is, the ideal of an art of living in which the pleasures and exigencies of life attain the perfection of a successful balance, as is the case in a work of art, best embodies the intuition of an aesthetic-expressive subjectivity: "We must ground, produce and order ourselves like a work of art."[49] The idea of an aesthetic of existence is characterized not by authenticity but by creativity, not by a code of rules but by style.

The intuition of the aesthetic of existence complements the theses that Foucault advocated in the 1970s regarding intellectuals and the insurrection of subjugated knowledges. Now as ever, social movements and the potential for self-realization, which counter existing normalizing impulses, are of central importance:

> The newer liberation movements suffer from their inability to find a principle on the basis of which they can work out a new ethics. They require an ethics and yet all they find is an ethics that is based on an ostensibly scientific knowledge of the self, of desire, and of the unconscious.[50]

Instead, reappropriation of pre-Christian ethics should provide the most appropriate instrument for the self-understanding of social movements.[51] Admittedly the emphasis here shifts from the political level of social confrontations to that of individual life plans, the political relevance of which must be understood indirectly, via gradual cultural processes. Here as well Foucault's theory proves to be a sensitive measure for the changes in the Zeitgeist of Western countries, where the retreat from politics is accompanied by an increase in "private" and aesthetic efforts at self-actualization.

> We believed, for example, that we could not change anything in our social and family life without having to simultaneously transform our economy, democracy, etc. I think we must free ourselves from the view that a necessary or analytic connection exists between ethics and social, economic or political structures. This does not mean that no relations at all exist between them. But that these relations are changeable.[52]

Who could seriously argue against such a statement today? My only corrective is this: The assertion that the private sphere indirectly depends on social conditions must not result in a reduction of the individual to the mere ability to creatively plan a new lifestyle without taking into account the individual's interactive dimension as a socialized being.

After a sincere and lifelong process of revising his views, the thinker of the "end of the individual," found in the early writings, turns to a form of extreme subjectivism that obscures the socialization problematic.

Chapter Six

Concluding Remarks

In the course of this discussion it has been shown that two crucial transformations of Bachelard's epistemology serve as the point of departure for Foucault's approach.

First of all, Foucault *expands* the sphere of application for the methods of historical epistemology. He does this by transposing Bachelard's critique of the epistemological subject-object line of questioning from the horizon of the natural sciences to the analysis of the history of culture and of social structure. As has been shown, even the more recent writings on antiquity can be interpreted as the further development of what is ultimately an epistemological problematic, in which introspection repeats the substantialist fallacy of traditional epistemology. Of course, the price of such a transformation is a grave failure to appreciate the distinction between the domain of nature and the symbolically prestructured world of culture. Foucault is unable to take into account the reconstructive method of the human sciences because his theoretical apparatus stems from the tension between traditional epistemology and the sciences of experience found in Bachelard, and he develops his critique of the human sciences on this basis.[1] The expansion of an epistemology that is critical of knowledge to include the human sciences also means that Foucault's theory adopts a related motif of Bachelard's: his rejection of the foundation problematic. This takes the form of a stubborn refusal to provide the normative grounds of his theory even though this refusal undermines his whole approach.

Secondly, with the historical a priori Foucault introduces a concept that is well suited to act as the *functional equivalent* of Bachelard's *spirit*. Foucault's entire course of thought (with the exception of his final writings on antiquity) could be defined as a history of his attempts to theorize the historical a priori. The declaration that the dream, madness, *episteme*, discourse, and power seem to be connected by a red thread when they are viewed as a series of transformations of the concept of the historical a priori is much more interesting when it is analyzed against the background of Bachelard's concept of spirit. For then it can be seen that all these conceptualizations result from the stubborn and repeatedly frustrated project of trying to retain the epistemological status of creative spirit without, however, reformulating it with the concepts of a philosophy of consciousness.

The unfeasibility of these endeavors is attested to not only by this study but by Foucault himself, who tacitly relinquishes this problematic, and with it the decisive core of the greater part of his work, in volumes 2 and 3 of *The History of Sexuality*.

The fact that I characterize as unsuccessful both of the transformations of Bachelard's work addressed here should not obscure their impact. What Foucault thereby recognizes, in any case, is the urgency of overcoming a philosophy of the subject. This task is one that most philosophical currents of this century have taken into account and that Foucault, with his masterful passages about the aporias of the human sciences, points out with particular clarity. In addition, the adoption of semiological and archaeological concepts by the structuralism of the 1960s indicates that Foucault, in his search for a new philosophical paradigm, took language to be central to his investigation.

The fact that Foucault, despite these approaches, was still unable to find a proper "escape from a philosophy of the subject" and was still unable to consider communicative alternatives can be attributed to the ambivalence and the systematic bottlenecks that adoption of Bachelard's approach necessarily entailed. This investigation repeatedly brought these difficulties to light. Foucault is able to criticize the self-referentiality of the human sciences and later, the related paradigm of the will to knowledge, and thus transcend the boundaries of the philosophy of the subject because he proceeds from the premise of the historical a priori, the changing configurations of which pull the rug out from under the self-referential foundation of a philosophy of the subject. The decisive step beyond the mentalist paradigm cannot be completed, however, because the historical a priori cannot plausibly reshape the features of Bachelard's creative spirit into its post-philosophy-of-the-subject form, be that in the form of semiology or of a theory of power. Thus, the definition of the central concept, that is, the historical a priori, remains theoretically incomplete; it shares the status of Bachelard's romantic spirit.

Foucault is positioned between the mentalistic and linguistic paradigms,[2] as it were; he is in search of a "postmodern" theory which, however, repeatedly returns him to the influence of the decidedly "modern" features that mark Bachelard's romanticism.

Deleuze has characterized Foucault's thought as "romantic positivism."[3] In trying to analyze this peculiar form of positivism, this work was able to more closely specify several features of Foucault's "anti-science," features that, like Bachelard's "applied rationalism," are characterized by a rejection of truth claims in favor of the creative production of new cultural contents. As indicated, Foucault understands himself as an empirical scientist (or technologist); his conception of rationality is satisfied with understanding his writings as "effects."

On that score, an important continuity in Foucault's thought can be ascertained that can be traced back to his first essay of 1954. In that essay cultural phenomena are treated as problems of style. In his later works Foucault no longer speaks of "style," but one could hardly find a better term to describe the ends and means posited by the struggles found in his theory of society; the art of living that is central to his final investigations; and even his own theoretical production, that is, the "effects" that it should call forth.

Such a reduction of cultural phenomena and of theory itself to mere problems of style, by its very one-sidedness, makes manifest particularly suggestive tendencies towards an aesthetic-expressive rationalization of modern societies. Yet this clearly does not alter the fact that completing the aestheticization of theory[4] in Foucault's romantic positivism—if consistently thought through—would amount to constructing theory itself, despite intentions to the contrary.

Nonetheless, Foucault is sufficiently ambiguous that, in a kaleidoscope of ambivalences, one can find theoretical rigor and critical engagement next to effects and problems of style, and scientific discipline and relentless self-critique next to a critique of reason. Perhaps for this reason not only his substantive investigations but his philosophy as a whole always offers new food for thought.

In this sense, volumes 2 and 3 of *The History of Sexuality*, as well as the final scattered essays and interviews, put the seal on his thought, in a manner of speaking. These writings, with their unsystematic, open-ended character and unforeseen developments, offer readers a tool, in Foucault's sense of the term, that each person can use for further projects.

Notes

Introduction

1. See A. Schmidt, *History and Structure: An Essay on Hegelian-Marxist and Structuralist Theories of History*, trans. J. Herf (Cambridge: MIT Press, 1981) on the anti-humanism critique. L. Ferry and A. Renault are concerned with a critique of anti-humanism in France. See *Antihumanistisches Denken. Gegen die französischen Meisterphilosophen* (Munich and Vienna, 1987). I must admit, however, that in some regards, such as its assessment of the student movement of 1968, I do not find this work convincing.

2. This concept stems from J. F. Lyotard, *The Postmodern Condition*, trans. G. Bennington (Minneapolis: University of Minnesota Press, 1984). On postmodernism see *Postmoderne. Zeichen eines kulturellen Wandels*, ed. A. Huyssen and K. R. Scherpe (Reinbeck bei Hamburg, 1986).

3. J. Habermas, *The Philosophical Discourse of Modernity*, trans. Frederick G. Lawrence (Cambridge: Polity Press, 1990), pg. 238ff; A. Honneth, *The Critique of Power*, trans. Kenneth Baynes (Cambridge: MIT Press, 1991).

4. One example: To the requirement that one be competent in that about which one speaks, one can always reply: "On the basis of which competence does one decide about competence?" To the question: "From where do you speak?" one can always answer: "Follow my voice and you will reach me!" S. Natoli, "Giochi di verita. L'epistemologia di Michel Foucault" in *Effeto Foucault*, ed. P. A. Rovatti (Milano, 1986), pg. 107f.

5. See D. Lecourt, "For a Critique of Epistemology" in *Marxism and Epistemology*, trans. B. Brewster (London, 1975); and E. Balibar, "From Bachelard to Althusser: The Concept of 'Epistemological Break'" in *Economy and Society*, vol. 7, no. 3 (1978), pg. 207ff.

6. G. Deleuze called attention to R. Roussel's influence on Foucault in G. Deleuze, *Foucault*, trans. Séan Hand (Minneapolis: University of Minnesota Press, 1988), pg. 47ff. Also see M. Foucault, *Raymond Roussel* (Paris: 1963).

7. M. Frank, *What Is Neostructuralism?*, trans. S. Wilke and R. Gray (Minneapolis: University of Minnesota Press, 1989), pg. 87ff.

Chapter 1

1. I am indebted to the comprehensive anthology of Bachelard's writings edited and annotated by G. Sertoli for my introduction to Bachelard's collected works. See *La ragione scientifica* (Verona, 1974). See the introduction by F. Dagognet, *Bachelard* (Paris, 1972), as well as the introduction by F. Lo Piparo to the Italian collection of Bachelard's writings, *Epistemologia* (Bari, 1975).

2. The article by R. Bhaskar is an exception here. See "Feyerabend and Bachelard. Two Philosophies of Science," *New Left Review* 94 (1975), pg. 31ff.

3. Above all see D. Lecourt's works, "For a Critique of Epistemology," and D. Lecourt and G. Canguilhem, *L'epistemologia di Gaston Bachelard* (Milano, 1974).

4. With regard to this point see W. Lepenies' "Introduction" to the German edition of G. Bachelard, *Die Bildung des wissenschaftlichen Geistes* (Frankfurt/M., 1978).

5. German has two terms for epistemology, "Erkenntnistheorie" and "Epistemologie." The former is used by Privitera to designate the epistemology of the philosophical tradition, the latter to designate Bachelard's form of epistemology, which, Bachelard contends, has been brought to the standard of the sciences. When it is necessary to distinguish between the two

I have rendered "Erkenntnistheorie" with "traditional epistemology" and "Epistemologie" with "critical epistemology." Trans.

6. G. Bachelard, *Le rationalisme appliqué* (Paris, 1949), pg. 79.

7. G. Bachelard, *The New Scientific Spirit* (Boston: Beacon Press, 1984), pp. 136–7.

8. I will return to the concept of the epistemological obstacle in section 4 of this chapter.

9. G. Bachelard, "L'actualité de l'histoire des sciences," in *L'engagement rationaliste* (Paris, 1972), pg. 142. [For translations from the French I thank Bruce Milem. Trans.]

10. See G. Canguilhem on the topic of discontinuity in the history of the sciences. *Wissenschaftsgeschichte und Epistemologie* (Frankfurt/M., 1979), pg. 7ff.

11. See G. Bachelard, *La formation de l'esprit scientifique* (Paris, 1938), pg. 8ff.

12. Ibid., pg. 9.

13. G. Bachelard, *Ausgewählte Texte* (Frankfurt/M., Berlin, Vienna, 1974), pg. 221.

14. G. Bachelard, "L'actualité de l'histoire des sciences," in *L'engagement rationaliste*, pg. 141.

15. G. Bachelard, *Ausgewählte Texte*, pg. 216.

16. G. Bachelard, *The New Scientific Spirit*, pg. 108. Obviously Bachelard is not the only thinker who has found the developments of modern physics important for philosophy. It is surprising that no bridges have been built between, for example, Popper's and Bachelard's theories.

17. Ibid., pg. 134.

18. G. Bachelard, *La formation de l'esprit scientifique*, pg. 14.

19. G. Bachelard, *The Philosophy of No: A Philosophy of the New Scientific Mind*, trans. G. C. Waterston (New York: Orion Press, 1968), pg. 8.

20. See G. Bachelard, *The New Scientific Spirit*, pg. 138ff.

21. See G. Bachelard, *Le rationalisme appliqué*, pg. 119ff.

22. Ibid., pg. 121.

23. Ibid.

24. Ibid., pg. 60.

25. Ibid., pg. 30.

26. Ibid., pg. 119ff.

27. See, for example, the historical analysis of the changes in meaning of the word "sponge" in G. Bachelard, *La formation de l'esprit scientifique*, pg. 73ff.

28. See H. Brühmann's critique in *Der Begriff des Hundes bellt nicht* (Wiesbaden, 1980), pg. 197ff.

29. G. Bachelard, *La dialectique de la durée* (Paris, 1950), pg. 7.

30. Ibid., pg. 130.

31. Ibid.

32. Ibid., pg. 131.

33. Ibid.

34. Ibid., pg. ix.

35. Ibid., pg. 67.

36. Ibid., pg. 6.

37. See *La ragione scientifica*, ed. G. Sertoli, pg. 444ff. As striking as Nietzsche's influence on Bachelard's collected work is, Bachelard's originality with regard to his idealistic metaphysics remains undisputed.

38. G. Bachelard, *The New Scientific Spirit*, pg. 175ff.

39. This characterization is from J. Hyppolite, "Gaston Bachelard ou le romantisme de l'intelligence" in *Hommage à Gaston Bachelard* (Paris, 1957), pg. 1ff.

40. See G. Canguilhem, *Wissenschaftsgeschichte und Epistemologie*, pg. 21.

41. G. Bachelard, *The New Scientific Spirit*, pg. 171.

42. Bachelard concerns himself with this topic in his book *The Philosophy of No.*

43. One of the most striking features of Bachelard's thought is its doubled character. Next to epistemological writings one finds a series of writings that are concerned with dreams, poetry, and with the imaginative products of the human mind in general. This duality of interests can be seen in his biography, which can be divided up into clear periods that alternate between the two thematic areas. See B. Waldenfels on Bachelard's work. *Phänomenologie in Frankreich* (Frankfurt/M., 1983), pg. 356ff.

44. See G. Bachelard, *La formation de l'esprit scientifique,* pg. 15.

45. Ibid., pg. 14.

46. With regard to the relation between science and epistemological obstacles Bachelard develops the idea of "recurrence" in the history of science. See M. Fichant, "Die Idee einer Wissenschaftsgeschichte," in M. Fichant and M. Pêcheux, *Überlegungen zur Wissenschaftsgeschichte* (Frankfurt/M., 1977), pg. 76ff.

47. G. Bachelard, *La formation de l'esprit scientifique,* pg. 251.

48. Ibid., pg. 14.

49. Lecourt develops an interpretation of epistemological obstacles as ideology out of this. See D. Lecourt and G. Canguilhem, *L'epistemologia di Gaston Bachelard.*

50. G. Bachelard, *La dialectique de la durée,* pg. 9.

51. G. Bachelard, *La formation de l'esprit scientifique,* pg. 252.

52. G. Bachelard, *The Philosophy of No,* pg. 11.

53. M. Vadée, *Epistemologie oder Philosophie? Zu Bachelards neuem epistemologischen Idealismus* (Frankfurt/M., 1979).

54. J. Hyppolite, "Gaston Bachelard ou le romantisme de l'intelligence" in *Hommage à Gaston Bachelard,* pg. 25.

55. Ibid., pg. 14.

56. Ibid.

Chapter 2

1. D. Lecourt, "For a Critique of Epistemology" in *Marxism and Epistemology*, trans. B. Brewster (London, 1975), pg. 187ff. In addition see J. Piaget, *Le structuralisme* (Paris, 1968), pg. 108ff.; and W. von Rahden, "Epistemologie und Wissenschaftskritik" in *Konsequenzen kritischer Wissenschaftstheorie*, ed. C. Hubig and W. von Rahden (Berlin and New York, 1978), pg. 162ff.

2. Numerous studies analyze the relationship of Nietzsche and Foucault. Among them see H. Fink-Eitel, "Foucaults Analytik der Macht" in *Die Austreibung des Geistes aus den Geisteswissenschaften*, ed. F. A. Kittler (Paderborn, 1980); and P. Rippel and H. Münkler, "Der Diskurs und die Macht" in *Politische Vierteljahresschrift* 23, Heft 2 (1982), pg. 115ff.

3. M. Frank argues in this way. See *What Is Neostructuralism?*, pg. 87ff.

4. See H. L. Dreyfus and P. Rabinow, *Michel Foucault: Beyond Structuralism and Hermeneutics* (Chicago: University of Chicago Press, 1982); J. Habermas, *The Philosophical Discourse of Modernity*, pg. 238ff; A. Honneth, *The Critique of Power*, trans. K. Baynes (Cambridge: MIT Press, 1991), pg. 105ff.; P. Veyne, *Der Eisberg der Geschichte* (Berlin, 1981).

5. On this topic see *La ragione scientifica*, ed. G. Sertoli, pg. 9ff.

6. Ibid., pg. 445.

7. J. Hyppolite, "Gaston Bachelard ou le romantisme de l'intelligence," pg. 25.

8. D. Lecourt, "For a Critique of Epistemology"; E. Balibar, "From Bachelard to Althusser: The Concept of 'Epistemological Break.'"

9. H. Brühmann, *Der Begriff des Hundes bellt nicht*.

10. *La ragione scientifica*, ed. G. Sertoli.

11. J. Hyppolite, "Gaston Bachelard ou le romantisme de l'intelligence"; M. Vadée, *Epistemologie oder Philosophie? Zu Bachelards neuem epistemologischem Idealismus*.

12. L. Binswanger, *Le rêve et l'existence* (Paris, 1954). Foucault's foreword to this piece was translated into English by Forrest Williams under the name "Dream, Imagination and Existence." See the *Review of Existential Psychology and Psychiatry* vol. XIX, No. 1 (1984–5). [Trans.]

13. M. Foucault, "Dream, Imagination and Existence," pg. 35.

14. Ibid., pg. 34.

15. Ibid., pg. 35.

16. Ibid., pg. 43.

17. Ibid., pg. 45ff.

18. Ibid., pg. 47.

19. Ibid., pg. 57.

20. Ibid., pg. 59.

21. The motif of the imaginary is quite pronounced in the French tradition. It can be found in various forms in Lacan and Bourdieu, among others, and leaves a readily discernable mark on Castoriadis's thought in particular. See C. Castoriadis, *The Imaginary Institution of Society*, trans. K. Blamey (Cambridge: MIT Press, 1987).

22. I am taking this definition from M. Ferraris's interesting work, *Differenze. La filosofia francese dopo lo strutturalismo* (Milano, 1981), pg. 137ff., which treats Foucault's theory in connection with that of Deleuze.

23. I will return to this topic in the section on "Statement, Discourse, Rules of Formation" in chapter 3.

24. M. Foucault, "Dream, Imagination and Existence," pg. 71.

25. Ibid., pg. 74.

26. See M. Ferraris, *Differenze*, pg. 137ff.

27. See J. Habermas on this topic. *Theory of Communicative Action*, vol. 1, trans. T. McCarthy (Boston: Beacon Press, 1984), pg. 22ff.

28. Ibid., pg. 19ff.

29. H. L. Dreyfus and P. Rabinow, *Michel Foucault: Beyond Structuralism and Hermeneutics*, pg. xvii. Not *Being and Time* but Heidegger's later works, especially the "Letter on Humanism" (in *Basic Writings*, ed. D. Krell [New York: Harper & Row, 1977]) which contains the famous Sartre critique, played an important role in the attempts of the young Foucault and others of his generation to break free from the topics that dominated the French discussion in the 1950s. In my view this is insufficient to argue, with regard to an author like Foucault, that he appropriated motifs relevant to his theory from Heidegger. His method, style, and contents are too strongly marked by a scientific, even positivistic, spirit for the search for far-reaching parallels to prove fruitful.

30. B. Waldenfels, *Phänomenologie in Frankreich*, pg. 441f. and 513ff.

31. See Deleuze on Foucault's transition from phenomenology to epistemology. *Foucault*, trans. S. Hand (Minneapolis: University of Minnesota Press, 1988).

32. H. Kocyba suggests a different interpretation in *Die reine Beschreibung diskursiver Ereignisse. Phänomenologie und Diskursanalyse bei Michel Foucault*, an unpublished manuscript (Frankfurt/M., 1986).

33. To my mind this is the decisive argument against Waldenfels's interpretation. See note 30 above.

34. M. Foucault, *Madness and Civilization*, trans. R. Howard (New York: Vintage Books, 1973).

35. M. Foucault, *Mental Illness and Psychology*, trans. A. Sheridan (Berkeley: University of California Press, 1987).

36. Ibid., pg. 74.

37. Ibid., pg. 85.

38. Ibid., pg. 74.

39. See J. Habermas on this topic. *The Philosophical Discourse of Modernity*, pg. 238.

40. "For a long time I was tormented by a conflict between a passion for Blanchot and Bataille on the one hand, and an interest in certain positive studies such as those by Dumézil and Lévi-

Strauss on the other." "Paolo Caruso. Gespräch mit Michel Foucault" in *Von der Subversion des Wissens* (Frankfurt/M., Berlin, Vienna, 1978), pg. 24.

41. See J. Habermas on the problem of self-referentiality in the philosophy of the subject. *The Philosophical Discourse of Modernity*, pg. 238ff.

42. M. Foucault, *The Order of Things*, trans. A. Sheridan. (New York: Vintage Books, 1973), pg. 303ff.

43. Ibid., pg. 320.

44. Ibid., pg. 341. (Emphasis added.)

45. See J. Habermas on the reconstructive sciences, *Erkenntnis und Interesse* (Frankfurt/M., 1983), pg. 411ff, and *Moral Consciousness and Communicative Action*, trans. C. L. Lenhardt and S. W. Nicholsen (Cambridge: Polity Press, 1990), pg. 21ff.

46. See J. Habermas, *The Philosophical Discourse of Modernity*, pg. 238ff. and especially 296ff.

47. M. Foucault, *The Order of Things*, pg. 379.

48. Ibid., pp. 381–2.

49. Ibid., pg. 382f.

50. Ibid., pg. 382.

51. Ibid., pg. 383.

52. M. Foucault, *The Archaeology of Knowledge*, trans. A. Sheridan. (New York: Pantheon, 1972), pg. 15.

Chapter 3

1. See S. Toulmin, *Human Understanding* (Princeton: Princeton University Press, 1972), pg. 96.

2. See D. Lecourt on this topic, "For a Critique of Epistemology," pg. 189ff.

3. See M. Foucault, *The Archaeology of Knowledge*, pg. 46 and pg. 117.

4. Ibid., pg. 6.

5. M. Foucault, "Theatrum Philosophicum" in *Language, Counter-Memory, Practice*, ed. Donald F. Bouchard (Ithaca: Cornell University Press, 1977), pg. 165ff.

6. On the topic of purity see G. Bachelard, *La formation de l'esprit scientifique;* and L. Althusser and E. Balibar, *Reading Capital*, trans. B. Brewster (London, 1979). In the foreword Althusser discusses the problem from the same epistemological perspective and with the same gold metaphor.

7. M. Foucault, *The Archaeology of Knowledge*, pg. 7.

8. M. Foucault, "On the Archaeology of the Sciences" in *Theoretical Practice* 3 (4) (1971).

9. M. Foucault, *The Archaeology of Knowledge*, pg. 28.

10. Ibid., pg. 27.

11. See M. Foucault, "Truth and Power" in *Power/Knowledge*, ed. C. Gordon (New York: Pantheon, 1980), pg. 114.

12. M. Foucault, *The Archaeology of Knowledge*, pg. 38.

13. Ibid., pg. 31ff.

14. Ibid., pg. 40ff.

15. I will come back to this. See M. Foucault, *The Archaeology of Knowledge* on this topic, pg. 113.

16. Ibid., pg. 40ff.

17. Ibid., pg. 50ff.

18. Ibid., pg. 56ff.

19. Ibid., pg. 64ff.

20. Chapters 3, 4, and 5 of *The Archaeology of Knowledge* can be understood as referring to *Madness and Civilization, The Birth of the Clinic, The Order of Things*, and the later studies on power, respectively. See pg. 65 of *The Archaeology of Knowledge* as well.

21. M. Foucault, *The Archaeology of Knowledge*, pg. 37.

22. Ibid., pg. 100.

23. See A. Honneth on this topic, *The Critique of Power*, pg. 132ff.

24. Foucault addressed speech act theory. His critique of the approach of speech act theory, however, was based on a misunderstanding, in my opinion. Namely, one cannot take the entire text of an oath or a contract as a speech act, as Foucault assumes (*The Archaeology of Knowledge*, pg. 83ff). For a taxonomy of illocutionary acts, see J. Searle, *Expression and Meaning* (New York: Cambridge University Press, 1979), pg. 1ff; and J. Habermas, *The Theory of Communicative Action*, vol. 1, pg. 319ff.

25. See V. Descombes on the role of mathematics in French structuralism, *Le même et l'autre* (Paris, 1979), pg. 103ff.

26. M. Foucault, *The Archaeology of Knowledge*, pp. 37 and 38.

27. Ibid., pg. 116.

28. Ibid., pg. 38.

29. Ibid., pg. 116.

30. C. Lévi-Strauss, *Structural Anthropology*, vol. 1, trans. C. Jacobson and B. Grundfest Schoepf (New York: Basic Books, 1963), pg. 65.

31. M. Foucault, "Réponse au Cercle d'Epistémologie," *Cahiers pour l'Analyse* 9 (1968), pg. 65. [The English translation of this text, "On the Archaeology of the Sciences," does not contain this passage. Trans.]

32. Ibid., pg. 127.

33. M. Foucault, *The Archaeology of Knowledge*, pg. 182.

34. M. Foucault, "On the Archaeology of the Sciences," pg. 127.

35. See the essay from I. Lakatos, "History of Science and Its Rational Reconstructions," *Boston Studies in the Philosophy of Science* vol. VIII (Dordrecht, 1971), pg. 91ff.

36. M. Foucault, "On the Archaeology of the Sciences," pg. 125.

37. T. Kuhn, *The Structure of Scientific Revolutions* (Chicago: University of Chicago Press, 1970).

38. M. Foucault, *The Archaeology of Knowledge*, pg. 49.

39. M. Foucault, "Dream, Imagination and Existence," pg. 74.

Chapter 4

1. M. Foucault, *The Archaeology of Knowledge*, pg. 154.

2. M. Foucault, "The Discourse on Language" in *The Archaeology of Knowledge*. This lecture was originally held at the College de France.

3. Ibid., pg. 218.

4. Ibid.

5. M. Foucault, "Theatrum Philosophicum," pg. 165ff.

6. Points of connection shared with critical theory and Nietzsche are particularly noticeable in this period of Foucault's thought. (M. Horkheimer and T. Adorno, *The Dialectic of Enlightenment*, trans. J. Cumming. New York: Continuum Publishing Co., 1987.) Compare A. Honneth on this topic: "Foucault et Adorno. Deux formes d'une critique de la modernité" in *Critique*, nos. 471–2 (1986).

7. M. Foucault, "Theatrum Philosophicum," pg. 181ff.

8. Ibid., pg. 168.

9. See "The Dream, Madness, and the Critique of Psychology" in chapter 2 above.

10. M. Foucault, "The Discourse on Language," pg. 219.

11. M. Foucault, "Power and Sex: An Interview," *Telos* no. 32 (Summer 1977), pg. 158.

12. M. Foucault, *Discipline and Punish*, trans. A. Sheridan (New York: Vintage Books, 1979).

13. M. Foucault, "Nietzsche, Genealogy, History" in *Language, Counter-Memory, Practice*, ed. D. F. Bouchard (Ithaca: Cornell University Press, 1977), pg. 139ff. In a recent interview ("The Ethics of Care for the Self as a Practice of Human Freedom," trans. J. D. Gauthier, S. J., *Philosophy and Social Criticism* 12

[1987], pp. 112–131), Foucault also indicates that there is a dualism in the concept of power. He talks, albeit unsystematically, about power and domination. Unfortunately I was unable to take up the subject matter of this interview in my own discussion.

14. Regarding the centrality of this essay see H. L. Dreyfus and P. Rabinow, *Michel Foucault: Beyond Structuralism and Hermeneutics*, pg. 106.

15. M. Foucault, "Nietzsche, Genealogy, History," pg. 147.

16. Ibid., pg. 148.

17. Ibid.

18. Ibid.

19. On this point see the written version of a lecture series held in 1976: M. Foucault, *Vom Licht des Krieges. Zur Geburt der Geschichte* (Berlin, 1986). Also see M. Foucault, "War in the Filigree of Peace." Course Summary in *Oxford Literary Review* 4:2 (1980), pg. 15f.

20. M. Foucault, "Nietzsche, Genealogy, History," pg. 150.

21. H. L. Dreyfus and P. Rabinow, *Michel Foucault: Beyond Structuralism and Hermeneutics*, pg. 108.

22. Foucault refers to this problem repeatedly. See *Discipline and Punish*, pg. 220ff., in which he writes about the reciprocal effect between the "accumulation of men" and the "accumulation of capital," as well as his minor writings, such as "Precisazioni sul potere. Risposta ad alcuni critici," in *aut aut* 167–168 (1978).

23. The first implicit correctives can be found in the lectures from January 7 and 14, 1976 (in M. Foucault, *Power/Knowledge*, pg. 78ff.), and explicit correctives can be found in volumes 2 and 3 of *The History of Sexuality*.

24. M. Foucault, "Nietzsche, Genealogy, History," pg. 150.

25. The essay on Nietzsche, in my view, should be read in this way.

26. M. Foucault, *Discipline and Punish*, pg. 74.

27. Ibid., pg. 26.

28. Ibid., pg. 194.

29. I borrow both the concept of a "philosophy of consciousness" and the analysis of its aporetic aspects from J. Habermas, *The Philosophical Discourse of Modernity*. In particular look at pg. 294ff. and pg. 296.

30. M. Foucault, *Discipline and Punish*, pg. 24.

31. Ibid., pg. 74.

32. Ibid., pg. 200.

33. Ibid., pg. 203.

34. Ibid., pg. 204.

35. Even the idea of the panopticon can be traced back to one of Bachelard's intuitions, though one that was admittedly peripheral to his project. In a manuscript about candlelight he describes the disciplinary relation between the one who stands in the light and the one who observes from the darkness. "The solitary dreamer who feels that he himself is kept under surveillance begins to survey his surveillant. He conceals his own lamp in order to expose that of the other." G. Bachelard, *La fiamma di una candela* (Rome: 1981), pg. 62.

36. M. Foucault, *The History of Sexuality*, vol. 1, trans. R. Hurley (New York: Vintage Books, 1980).

37. M. Foucault, *Discipline and Punish*, pg. 29f.

38. On the problematic relation between power and knowledge, see J. Habermas, *The Philosophical Discourse of Modernity*, pg. 272.

39. M. Foucault, "Nietzsche, Genealogy, History," pg. 153.

40. Ibid.

41. The fact that phenomenology is one of the most important targets of Foucault's critique is due not only to his adoption of Bachelard's anti-phenomenological motifs, but more generally to a certain weariness with the major interpreters of phenomenology in France (Merleau-Ponty or Sartre) who left their mark on Foucault's entire generation (the structuralist or post-structuralist generation). Regarding the changes in France at the time of struc-

turalism see B. Waldenfels, *Phänomenologie in Frankreich*, pg. 486ff.

42. E. Husserl, *The Crisis of the European Sciences and Transcendental Phenomenology*, trans. D. Carr (Evanston: Northwestern University Press, 1970).

43. M. Foucault, "Nietzsche, Genealogy, History," pg. 151.

44. M. Foucault, "Truth and Power," pg. 117.

45. M. Foucault, "Nietzsche, Genealogy, History," pg. 153.

46. One could translate the work "regime" with "heteronomously determined way of life" (*heteronom bestimmte Lebensweise*).

47. Foucault's and Bachelard's critiques of knowledge would be unimaginable without Nietzsche and his historical effect. See, for example, F. Nietzsche, *Erkenntnistheoretische Schriften* (Frankfurt/M., 1968). Even more important for marking the difference between the two is the allusion to Foucault's non-vitalistic attitude.

48. F. Nietzsche, "Aus dem Nachlass der Achtziger Jahre" in *Erkenntistheoretische Schriften*, pg. 197.

49. M. Foucault, "Nietzsche, Genealogy, History," pg. 155.

50. I return to this in the next few pages.

51. M. Foucault, "Truth and Power," pg. 115.

52. M. Foucault, "Power and Norm: Notes," in *Power, Truth, Strategy*, ed. M. Morris and P. Putton (Sydney, Australia: Feral Publications, 1979), pg. 59.

53. See A. Honneth, *The Critique of Power*, pg. 155, on this point.

54. M. Foucault, "Two Lectures" in *Power/Knowledge*, pg. 98.

55. A. Honneth offers a critical discussion of this topic in *The Critique of Power*, pg. 159ff. According to Deleuze's reading, knowledge relations, as described in the *Archaeology*, stabilize social contexts. See G. Deleuze, *Foucault*, pp. 75–76. It is still unclear, however, in what sense stratifications of knowledge can be said to exert a stabilizing influence on power practices.

56. M. Foucault, "Two Lectures," pg. 98.

57. See my discussion at the beginning of "The Semiologization of the Imaginary" in chapter 3.

Chapter 5

1. M. Foucault, *The Use of Pleasure*, trans. R. Hurley (New York: Pantheon, 1985) and *The Care of the Self*, trans. R. Hurley (New York: Pantheon, 1986).

2. M. Foucault, "Truth and Power," pg. 123.

3. Many of Foucault's theses could be compared with E. Goffman's analysis of "total institutions." *Asylums* (New York: Anchor Books, 1961).

4. "Structuralist holism" is how Dreyfus and Rabinow describe Foucault's approach during his semiological period. (*Michel Foucault: Beyond Structuralism and Hermeneutics*, pg. 55.)

5. See J. Habermas, "Reconstruction and Interpretation in the Social Sciences," in *Moral Consciousness and Communicative Action*, trans. C. L. Lenhardt and S. W. Nicholsen (Cambridge, England: Polity Press, 1990), pg. 21.

6. On human "doubling" see M. Foucault, *The Order of Things*, pg. 303ff.

7. M. Foucault, *The History of Sexuality*, pg. 21.

8. Ibid., pg. 98.

9. This is found in the previously cited interview with A. Fontana and P. Pasquino in *Power/Knowledge*, pg. 126ff.

10. Ibid., pg. 126.

11. See J. Habermas, *The Theory of Communicative Action*, vol. 2, pg. 351ff. Other conclusions about the role of the intellectual can be drawn from the change in the function of ideology, however. See J. Habermas, "Die Rolle des Intellektuellen," *Merkur* Heft 6, Nr. 448 (1986); and H. Brunkhorst's interesting study, *Die Intellektuelle im Land der Mandarine* (Frankfurt/M.,

1978). See H. Dubiel for a sociological view of the contemporary discussion on this topic, *Was ist Neokonservatismus?* (Frankfurt/M., 1985), pg. 105ff.

12. M. Foucault, *The History of Sexuality*, vol. 1, pg. 159.

13. M. Foucault, "Two Lectures" in *Power/Knowledge*, pg. 81.

14. Ibid., pg. 82.

15. On the problem of Foucault and normativity see N. Fraser, "Foucault on Modern Power: Empirical Insights and Normative Confusions," *Praxis International* I, no. 3 (1981), pg. 281ff.

16. See "Anti-Science" in chapter 2 above.

17. See "The Epistemological Obstacle" in chapter 1 above.

18. M. Foucault, "Two Lectures," pg. 82.

19. See "Interregional Rationalism and Discontinuity" in chapter 1 above.

20. M. Foucault, "Two Lectures," pg. 82f.

21. I borrow the term "applied rationalism" from the title of Bachelard's books. See "Interregional Rationalism and Discontinuity" in chapter 1 on this topic.

22. H. L. Dreyfus and P. Rabinow, *Michel Foucault: Beyond Structuralism and Hermeneutics*, pg. 221.

23. Ibid., pg. 124.

24. Ibid.

25. Foucault always criticized hermeneutics because he saw its understanding of interpretation as paradigmatic of the sterile search for the "true kernel" of a text or an intention. (See his critique of commentary in the introduction to *The Birth of the Clinic*, trans. A. M. S. Smith (New York: Vintage Books, 1975.) For all that he failed to see that Gadamer's *Truth and Method* already set the course by which intersubjective theory would overcome the very subject-object line of questioning (characteristic of a philosophy of the subject) against which his epistemology was directed.

26. M. Foucault, "Nietzsche, Genealogy, History," pg. 152.

27. Even the very Nietzchean-sounding formulation "will to knowledge" can be found in Bachelard.

28. M. Foucault, "Two Lectures," pg. 84.

29. Ibid.

30. See "Bachelard's Philosophy" in chapter 1 above.

31. For example, Foucault speaks of "effects" in his essay "Precisazioni sul potere. Risposta ad alcuni critici," pg. 11. He also expresses himself very clearly in this regard in a conversation with Lucette Finas. "I am well aware that I have never written anything but fictions. I do not mean to say, however, that truth is therefore absent. It seems to me that the possibility exists for fiction to function in truth, for a fictional discourse to induce effects of truth, and for bringing it about that a true discourse engenders or 'manufactures' something that does not as yet exist, that is, 'fictions' it. One 'fictions' history on the basis of a political reality that makes it true, one 'fictions' a politics not yet in existence on the basis of a historical truth." M. Foucault, "The History of Sexuality" in *Power/Knowledge*, pg. 193.

32. J. Habermas discusses Foucault's "politics of theory" in *The Philosophical Discourse of Modernity*, pg. 279.

33. P. K. Feyerabend, *Against Method: Outline of an Anarchistic Theory of Knowledge.* (London: NLB, 1975).

34. J. Habermas, *The Philosophical Discourse of Modernity*, pg. 257. Among the numerous studies about the political implications of Foucault's work, see N. Fraser, "Michel Foucault: A 'Young Conservative'?," *Ethics* vol. 96, no. 1(1985) pg. 165ff; C. Kammler, *Michel Foucault. Eine kritische Analyse seines Werks* (Bonn: 1986); and M. Poster, *Foucault, Marxism and History* (Cambridge: Polity Press, 1984).

35. See Foucault's essay on Kant "What Is Enlightenment?" in *The Foucault Reader*, ed. P. Rubinow (New York: Pantheon, 1984). In this essay Foucault describes his theory as "critical theory." He expresses a similar view with regard to the Frankfurt School in the interview with Gerard Raniet, "Structuralism and Post-Structuralism: An Interview with Michel Foucualt," *Telos*, no. 55 (1983), pg. 200.

36. See "Hidden Normativity" above.

37. M. Foucault, "The Subject and Power," in *Michel Foucault: Beyond Structuralism and Hermeneutics*, pg. 211.

38. See J. Habermas, *The Theory of Communicative Action*, vol. 2, pg. 3ff and his "Justice and Solidarity: On the Discussion Concerning Stage 6," in *The Moral Domain*, ed. T. Wren (Cambridge: MIT Press, 1990).

39. M. Foucault, *The Use of Pleasure*; and M. Foucault, *The Care of the Self*.

40. Here I have in mind M. Foucault's *Dispositive der Macht* and *Von der Subversion des Wissens*.

41. M. Foucault, *The Use of Pleasure*, pg. 8.

42. Ibid., pg. 11.

43. P. Pasquino drew the connection between the art of life in Foucault's final works and the problematic of leading one's life found in Weber. See "Foucault (1926–1984): la volontà di sapere," in *Quaderni piacentini* 14 (1984), pg. 53ff. Even more astonishing is his insistence that Foucault's thought develops along a linear path.

44. M. Foucault, *The Use of Pleasure*, pg. 11.

45. Ibid., pg. 12.

46. On his radical change with regard to the question of subjectivity see P. A. Rovatti, "Il luogo del soggetto" in his *Effeto Foucault* (Milano, 1986), pg. 71ff.

47. M. Foucault, *The Use of Pleasure*, pg. 11ff.

48. See "Bachelard's Philosophy" in chapter 1 above.

49. M. Foucault, *Von der Freundschaft* (Berlin, 1986), pg. 81.

50. Ibid., pg. 71.

51. C. Taylor criticizes the view that themes from antiquity, irrespective of the Christian tradition, can offer a serious cultural alternative to our Western tradition. "Foucault on Freedom and Truth" in *Philosophical Papers, Vol. 2: Philosophy and the Human Sciences* (Cambridge: Cambridge University Press, 1985).

52. M. Foucault, *Von der Freundschaft*, pg. 80.

Chapter 6

1. On reconstruction see J. Habermas, *Erkenntnis und Interesse*, pg. 411ff., and his "Reconstruction and Interpretation in the Social Sciences" in *Moral Consciousness and Communicative Action*, pg. 21.

2. I borrow this terminology from H. Schnädelbach, *Philosophie. Ein Grundkurs* (Reinbek bei Hamburg, 1985), pg. 36ff. K. O. Apel suggested a similar systematization of the philosophy of history even earlier. See K. O. Apel, "Transcendental Semiotics and the Paradigms of First Philosophy," *Philosophic Exchange* vol. 2, no. 4 (1978), pg. 3ff.

3. G. Deleuze, "Ein neuer Archivar" in G. Deleuze and M. Foucault, *Der Faden ist Gerissen*, pg. 73. Alessandro Fontana expresses a similar view in his "Introduzione" to the Italian edition of M. Foucault's *Nascita della clinica* (Torino, 1969), pg. xv.

4. In this sense M. Blanchot maintained that Foucault, counter to his own self-understanding, was ultimately an author. M. Blanchot, *Michel Foucault, vorgestellt von Maurice Blanchot* (Tübingen, 1987), pg. 18.

Bibliography

Althusser, Louis, and Balibar, Etienne. *Reading Capital.* Translated by Ben Brewster. London: New Left Books, 1970.

Apel, Karl-Otto. "Transcendental Semiotics and the Paradigms of First Philosophy." *Philosophic Exchange*, vol. 2, no. 4 (1978): 3ff.

Bachelard, Gaston. *Ausgewählte Texte.* Frankfurt/M., Berlin, Vienna: 1974.

———. *Die Bildung des wissenschaftlichen Geistes.* Frankfurt/M.: 1978.

———. *La dialectique de la durée.* Paris: 1950.

———. *L'engagement rationaliste.* Paris: 1972.

———. *Epistemologia.* Bari: 1975.

———. *La fiamma di una candela.* Rome: 1981.

———. *La formation de l'esprit scientifique.* Paris: 1938.

———. *The New Scientific Spirit.* Boston: Beacon Press, 1984.

———. *The Philosophy of No: A Philosophy of the New Scientific Mind.* Translated by G. C. Waterston. New York: Orion Press, 1968.

———. *The Psychoanalysis of Fire.* Translated by Alan C. M. Ross. Boston: Beacon Press, 1964.

———. *Le rationalisme appliqué.* Paris: 1949.

Balibar, Etienne. "From Bachelard to Althusser: The Concept of 'Epistemological Break.'" *Economy and Society*, vol. 7, no. 3 (1978): 207ff.

Bhaskar, R. "Feyerabend and Bachelard. Two Philosophies of Science." *New Left Review* 94 (1975): 31ff.

Binswanger, Ludwig. *Le rêve et l'existence.* Paris: 1954.

Blanchot, Maurice. *Michel Foucault, vorgestelltvon Maurice Blanchot.* Tübingen: 1987.

Brühmann, Horst. *Der Begriff des Hundes bellt nicht.* Wiesbaden: 1980.

Brunkhorst, Hauke. *Der Intellektuelle im Land der Mandarine.* Frankfurt/M.: 1978.

Canguilhem, Georges. *Wissenschaftsgeschichte und Epistemologie.* Frankfurt/M.: 1979.

Caruso, Paolo. "Gesprächmit Michel Foucault." In *Vonder Subversion des Wissens.* Frankfurt/M., Berlin, Vienna: 1978.

Castoriadis, Cornelius. *The Imaginary Institution of Society.* Translated by Kathleen Blamey. Cambridge: MIT Press, 1987.

Clark, Michael. *Michel Foucault. An Annotated Bibliography.* New York: Garland Press, 1983.

Dagognet, F. *Bachelard.* Paris: 1972.

Deleuze, Gilles. *Foucault.* Translated by Séan Hand. Minneapolis: University of Minnesota Press, 1988. "Ein neuer Archivar." In Gilles Deleuze and Michel Foucault, *Der Fadenist Gerissen.* Berlin: 1977.

Descombes, Vincent. *Le même et l'autre.* Paris: 1979.

Dionigi, R. *La "filosofia" come ostacolo epistemologico.* Padova: 1973.

Dreyfus, Hubert L., and Rabinow, Paul. *Michel Foucault: Beyond Structuralism and Hermeneutics.* Chicago: University of Chicago Press, 1982.

Dubiel, H. *Was ist Neokonservatismus?* Frankfurt/M.: 1985.

Ferraris, M. *Differenze. La filosofia francese dopo lo strutturalismo.* Milano: 1981.

Ferry, L., and Renault, A. *Antihumanistisches Denken. Gegen die franzözischen Meisterphilosophen*. Munich, Vienna: 1987.

Feyerabend, Paul. *Against Method: Outline of an Anarchistic Theory of Knowledge*. London: 1975.

Fichant, M., and Pêcheux, M. *Überlegungen zur Wissenschafts-geschichte*. Frankfurt/M.: 1977.

Fink-Eitel, Heinrich. "Foucaults Analytik der Macht." In *Die Austreibung des Geistes aus den Geisteswissenschaften*, edited by F. A. Kittler. Paderborn: 1980.

Fontana, A. "Introduzione" to M. Foucault, *Nascita della clinica. Il ruolo della medicina nella costituzione delle scienze umane*. Torino: 1969.

Foucault, Michel. *The Archaeology of Knowledge*. Translated by Alan Sheridan. New York: Pantheon Books, 1972.

———. "Eine Ästhetik der Existenz. Gespräch mit Alessandro Fontana." In *Von der Freundschaft*. West Berlin: 1986.

———. *The Birth of the Clinic*. Translated by Alan Sheridan. New York: Vintage Books, 1975.

———. *The Care of the Self: History of Sexuality*, vol. 3. Translated by R. Hurley. New York: Pantheon, 1986.

———. *Discipline and Punish*. Translated by Alan Sheridan. New York: Vintage Books, 1979.

———. "The Discourse on Language." In *The Archaeology of Knowledge*. Translated by Alan Sheridan. NY: Pantheon, 1972.

———. *Dispositive der Macht*. West Berlin: 1978.

———. "Dream, Imagination, and Existence." Translated by F. Williams. *Review of Existential Psychology and Psychiatry* 19 (1984–85): 29–78.

———. "The Ethics of Care for the Self as a Practice of Human Freedom." Translated by J. D. Gauthier, S.J. *Philosophy and Social Criticism* 12 (1987): 112–31.

——— . "The History of Sexuality." In *Power/Knowledge*, edited by C. Gordon. New York: Pantheon, 1980.

——— . *The History of Sexuality, Vol. I.: An Introduction.* Translated by R. Hurley. New York: Vintage Books, 1980.

——— . *Madness and Civilization.* Translated by Richard Howard. New York: Vintage Books, 1973.

——— . *Mental Illness and Psychology.* Translated by Alan Sheridan. Berkeley: University of California Press, 1987.

——— . "Nein zum König Sex. Gespräch mit Bernard-Henry Lévy." In *Dispositive der Macht.* West Berlin: 1978.

——— . "Nietzsche, Genealogy, History." In *Language, Counter-Memory, Practice*, edited by Donald F. Bouchard. Ithaca: Cornell University Press, 1977.

——— . "On Archaeology of the Sciences." *Theoretical Practice* 3(4) (1971).

——— . *The Order of Things.* Translated by Alan Sheridan. New York: Vintage Books, 1973.

——— . "An Overview of Work in Progress." In *Michel Foucault: Beyond Structuralism and Hermeneutics*, edited by Hubert L. Dreyfus and Paul Rabinow. Chicago: University of Chicago Press, 1982.

——— . "Power and Norm: Notes." In *Power, Truth, Strategy*, edited by M. Morris and P. Patton. Sydney: Feral Publications, 1979.

——— . "Power and Sex: An Interview." *Telos* no. 32 (Summer 1977).

"Precisazioni sul potere. Risposta ad alcuni critici." *aut aut* 167–168 (1978).

——— . *Raymond Roussel.* Paris: 1963.

——— . "Réponse au Cercle d'Épistémologie." *Cahiers pour l'Analyse* 9 (1968).

——— . "Structuralism and Post-Structuralism: An Interview with Michel Foucault." *Telos* 55 (1983).

———. "The Subject and Power." Afterword to Hubert L. Dreyfus and Paul Rabinow, *Michel Foucault: Beyond Structuralism and Hermeneutics*. Chicago: University of Chicago Press, 1982.

———. "Theatrum Philosophicum." In *Language, Countermemory, Practice*, edited by D. Borchard. Ithaca: Cornell University Press, 1977.

———. "Truth and Power." In *Power/Knowledge*, edited by C. Gordon. New York: Pantheon, 1980.

———. "Two Lectures." In *Power/Knowledge*, edited by C. Gordon. New York: Pantheon, 1980.

———. *The Use of Pleasure*. Translated by R. Hurley. New York: Pantheon, 1985.

———. *Von der Freundschaft*. Berlin: 1986.

———. *Von der Subversion des Wissens*. Frankfurt/M., Berlin, Vienna: 1978.

———. *Vom Licht des Krieges. Zur Geburt der Geschichte*. Berlin: 1986.

———. "War in the Filigree of Peace." *Oxford Literary Review* 4:2. (1980): 15ff.

———. "What is Enlightenment" in *The Foucault Reader*, edited by P. Rubinow (New York: Pantheon, 1984).

Frank, Manfred. *What Is Neostructuralism?* Translated by Sabine Wilke and Richard Gray. Minneapolis: University of Minnesota Press, 1989.

Fraser, Nancy. "Foucault on Modern Power: Empirical Insights and Normative Confusions." *Praxis International* I, no. 3 (1981).

———. "Michel Foucault: A 'Young Conservative'?" *Ethics*, vol. 96, no. 1 (1985).

Gadamer, Hans Georg. *Truth and Method*. Translated by Garret Barden and William Glen-Doepel. New York: Seabury Press, 1975.

Goffman, E. *Asylums*. New York: Anchor Books, 1961.

Habermas, Jürgen. *Erkenntnis und Interesse*. Frankfurt/M., 1983.

——— . "Justice and Solidarity: On the Discussion Concerning Stage 6" in *The Moral Domain*, edited by Thomas Wren (Cambridge: MIT Press, 1990).

——— . *Knowledge and Human Interests*. Translated by Jeremy Shapiro. Boston: Beacon Press, 1971.

——— . *Moral Consciousness and Communicative Action*. Translated by C. L. Lenhardt and S. W. Nicholsen. Cambridge, England: Polity Press, 1990.

——— . *The Philosophical Discourse of Modernity*. Translated by Frederick G. Lawrence. Cambridge: Polity Press, 1990.

——— . "Die Rolle des Intellektuellen." *Merkur* Heft 6, no. 448 (1986).

——— . *Theory of Communicative Action*, vol 1. Translated by Thomas McCarthy. Boston: Beacon Press, 1984.

——— . *Theory of Communicative Action*, vol. 2. Translated by Thomas McCarthy. Boston: Beacon Press, 1987.

Heidegger, Martin. *Being and Time*. Translated by John Macquarrie and Edward Robinson. New York: Harper, 1962.

——— . "Letter on Humanism." In *Basic Writings*, edited by David Krell. New York: Harper & Row, 1977.

Honneth, Axel. *The Critique of Power*. Translated by Kenneth Baynes. Cambridge: MIT Press, 1991.

——— . "Foucault et Adorno. Deux formes d'une critique de la modernité." *Critique* nos. 471–72 (1986).

Horkheimer, Max, and Adorno, Theodor. *The Dialectic of Enlightenment*. Translated by John Cumming. New York: Continuum, 1987.

Husserl, Edmund. *The Crisis of the European Sciences and Transcendental Phenomenology*. Translated by David Carr. Evanston, IL: Northwestern University Press, 1970.

Huyssen, Andreas, and Scherpe, Klaus R. *Postmoderne. Zeichen eines kulturellen Wandels*. Reinbeck bei Hamburg: 1986.

Hyppolite, Jean. "Gaston Bachelard ou le romantisme de l'intelligence." *Hommage à Gaston Bachelard.* Paris: 1957.

Kammler, Clemens. *Michel Foucault. Eine kritische Analyse seines Werks.* Bonn: 1986.

Kocyba, H. *Die reine Beschreibung diskursiver Ereignisse. Phänomenologie und Diskursanalyse bei Michel Foucault.* Unpublished manuscript. Frankfurt/M.: 1986.

Kuhn, Thomas. *The Structure of Scientific Revolutions.* Chicago: University of Chicago Press, 1970.

LaKatos, I. "History of Science and Its Rational Reconstructions." *Boston Studies in the Philosophy of Science,* vol. VIII (1971): 91ff.

Lecourt, Dominique. "For a Critique of Epistemology." Translated by Ben Brewster, in *Marxism and Epistemology.* London: 1975.

Lecourt, Dominique, and Canguilhem, Georges. *L'epistemologia di Gaston Bachelard.* Milano: 1974.

Lepenies, W. "Einleitung." *Die Bildung des wissenschaftlichen Geistes.* Frankfurt/M.: 1978.

Lévi-Strauss, Claude. *Structural Anthropology,* vol. I. Translated by Claire Jacobsen and Brooke Grundfest Schoepf. New York: Basic Books, 1963.

Lo Piparo, F. "Introduzione." To G. Bachelard, *Epistemologia.* Bari: 1975.

Lyotard, Jean Francois. *The Postmodern Condition.* Translated by Geoff Bennington. Minneapolis: University of Minnesota Press, 1984.

Natoli, S., *Ermeneutica genealogia. Filosofia a metodo in Nietzsche, Heidegger, Foucault.* Milano: 1981

———. "Giochi di verità. L'epistemologia di Michel Foucault." In *Effeto Foucault,* edited by P. A. Rovatti. Milano: 1986.

Nietzsche, Friedrich. *Erkenntnistheoretische Schriften.* Frankfurt/M.: 1968.

Pasquino, P. "Foucault (1926–1984): la volontà di sapere" in *Quaderni piacentini* 14 (1984): 53ff.

Piaget, Jean. *Le structuralisme*. Paris: 1968.

Poster, M. *Foucault, Marxism and History. Mode of Production versus Mode of Information*. Cambridge: Polity Press, 1984.

Rahden, W. von. "Epistemologie und Wissenschaftskritik." In *Konsequenzen kritischer Wissenschaftstheorie*, edited by C. Hubig and W. von Rahden. Berlin: 1978.

Rippel, P., and Münkler, H. "Der Diskurs und die Macht." *Politische Vierteljahresschrift* 23, Heft 2 (1982): 115ff.

Rovatti, Pier. Aldo., "Il luogo del soggetto." *Effeto Foucault*. Milano: 1986.

Schivelbusch, Wolfgang. *Lichtblicke. Zur Geschichte der künstlichen Helligkeit im 19. Jahrhundert*. Frankfurt/M.: 1986.

Schmidt, Alfred. *History and Structure: An Essay on Hegelian-Marxist and Structuralist Theories of History*. Translated by Jeffrey Herf. Cambridge: MIT Press, 1981.

Schnädelbach, H. "Philosophie." In *Philosophie. Ein Grundkurs*, edited by E. Martens and H. Schnädelbach. Reinbek bei Hamburg: 1985.

Searle, John. *Expression and Meaning: Studies in the Theory of Speech Acts*. New York: Cambridge University Press, 1979.

Sertoli, G. "Introduzione." In *La ragione scientifica*, edited by G. Sertoli. Verona: 1974.

Taylor, Charles. "Foucault on Freedom and Truth." In *Philosophical Papers, Vol. 2: Philosophy and the Human Sciences*. Cambridge: Cambridge University Press, 1985.

Toulmin, Stephen. *Human Understanding*. Princeton: Princeton University Press, 1972.

Vadée, Michel. *Epistemologie oder Philosophie? Zu Bachelards neuem epistemologischen Idealismus*. Frankfurt/M.: 1979.

Veyne, P. *Der Eisberg der Geschichte*. Berlin: 1981.

Waldenfels, Bernhard. *Phänomenologie in Frankreich*. Frankfurt/M.: 1983.

Index

Action, 77, 92-93, 94-95

Aesthetic of existence, xiv, 118-19, 122-25, 130, 149n.43

Althusser, Louis, xiii

Althusser School, xiii, 2, 30

Anthropology, 41; of expression, 31, 32, 34-36, 38, 60

Antiquity, 149n.51; and dreams, 32; ethics of, 124; Foucault's studies of, 119, 122-23

Anti-science, xii, xiii, xv, 42-47

Apodicity, 11-12, 107

Apollo, 72

Apparatus, 94-95, 101, 102, 109

Applied rationalism, 13-14, 112-16, 129-30. *See also* Regional knowledge

A priori. *See* Historical a priori

Archaeology, 129; choice of term, 51-52; and document/monument distinction, 50-51; and epistemological break, 62; and interpretive analytics, 112

Archaeology of Knowledge, The, xiv, 46, 49-52, 67-68, 78, 89, 97; on autonomy of discourse, 91, 95; on discursive formations and rules of formation, 54, 55, 57-59, 93-94; semiologization of the imaginary in, 59-61; on statements, 53-59, 68, 91, 93-94; and validity problematic, 61-65

Arithmetic, 7. *See also* Mathematics

Art of life. *See* Aesthetic of existence

Asceticism, 1, 22, 29-30, 107-8

Ascetic vitalism, 29-30

Autonomy of discourse, 91, 95

Bachelard, Gaston, 1-3, 64, 127-28; on constructions, 7-12, 16-17, 19-20, 29, 107, 113; critique of realism by, 7-8, 54-55, 56, 122; on discontinuities, 5, 14-18; on epistemological obstacles, 4, 18-22, 29-30, 61; on imagination, 19, 22-24, 30, 34, 135n.43; influence of, xiii-xiv, 2, 28; and panopticon, 144n.35; on regional ratio-